christmas gifts
UNDER $10

*T*ired *of enduring jammed shopping malls and paying high prices at Christmastime, only to end up with gifts that don't live up to your expectations? Now you can leave all that behind. With Christmas Gifts Under $10 at your fingertips, it's a cinch to craft more than 100 clever creations that will touch the hearts of your loved ones!*

Here's the challenge we gave our designers:

1. Develop great gifts that cost less than $10 each.

2. Shop in typical craft and discount stores.

3. Bring in your cash register receipts as proof of how much the average crafter can expect to spend.

We were amazed at the results! Who would have guessed that you could make such extraordinary gifts using inexpensive, ordinary supplies — and to do it so quickly and easily? This book is truly a one-of-a-kind treasury!

With our super-simple instructions, even beginners will be turning out memorable holiday gifts faster than Santa's elves. There are presents for all your favorite people ... festive fashions to wear throughout the holiday season ... thrifty little tokens that you can make lots of ... and yummy treats from your kitchen, attractively packaged and presented.

Best of all, you'll deliver every gift with a smile, knowing you've created just the right presents for everyone — without breaking your budget! Enjoy your merriest Christmas ever!

Anne Childs

LEISURE ARTS, INC.
Little Rock, Arkansas

christmas gifts UNDER $10

EDITORIAL STAFF

Vice President and Editor-in-Chief: Anne Van Wagner Childs
Executive Director: Sandra Graham Case
Editorial Director: Susan Frantz Wiles
Publications Director: Carla Bentley
Creative Art Director: Gloria Bearden
Senior Graphics Art Director: Melinda Stout

DESIGN
Design Director: Patricia Wallenfang Sowers
Designers: Katherine Prince Horton,
    Sandra Spotts Ritchie, Anne Pulliam Stocks,
    Linda Diehl Tiano, and Rebecca Sunwall Werle
Executive Assistant: Billie Steward

FOODS
Foods Editor: Celia Fahr Harkey, R.D.
Assistant Foods Editor: Jane Kenner Prather
Test Kitchen Home Economist: Rose Glass Klein
Test Kitchen Coordinator: Nora Faye Taylor

TECHNICAL
Managing Editor: Kathy Rose Bradley
Senior Technical Writer: Leslie Schick Gorrell
Technical Writer: Kimberly J. Smith
Technical Associates: Margaret F. Cox,
    Briget Julia Laskowski, and Joan Gessner Beebe

EDITORIAL
Managing Editor: Linda L. Trimble
Associate Editor: Robyn Sheffield-Edwards
Assistant Editors: Tammi Williamson Bradley,
    Terri Leming Davidson, and Darla Burdette Kelsay
Copy Editor: Laura Lee Weland

ART
Book/Magazine Graphics Art Director: Diane M. Hug
Senior Production Graphics Artist: Michael A. Spigne
Photography Stylists: Pam Choate, Sondra Daniel,
    Laura Dell, Aurora Huston, and Courtney Frazier Jone

PROMOTIONS
Managing Editors: Tena Kelley Vaughn
    and Marjorie Ann Lacy
Associate Editors: Steven M. Cooper, Dixie L. Morris,
    and Jennifer Leigh Ertl
Designer: Dale Rowett
Art Director: Linda Lovette Smart
Production Artist: Leslie Loring Krebs
Publishing Systems Administrator: Cindy Lumpkin
Publishing Systems Assistant: Susan Mary Gray

BUSINESS STAFF

Publisher: Bruce Akin
Vice President, Marketing: Guy A. Crossley
Marketing Manager: Byron L. Taylor
Print Production Manager: Laura Lockhart
Vice President and General Manager: Thomas L. Carlisle
Retail Sales Director: Richard Tignor

Vice President, Retail Marketing: Pam Stebbins
Retail Marketing Director: Margaret Sweetin
Retail Customer Service Manager: Carolyn Pruss
General Merchandise Manager: Russ Barnett
Vice President, Finance: Tom Siebenmorgen
Distribution Director: Ed M. Strackbein

Library of Congress Catalog Number 96-78950
International Standard Book Number 0-8487-4153-6

Table of Contents

GIFTS FOR ALL.....................................6

THE MORE THE MERRIER 42

FESTIVE FLAIR 68

CREATIVE CHRISTMAS KITCHEN 84

The stockings hang o'er fireplace glowing,
That tenderest hands with gifts shall fill,
Each token from the heart, bestowing
The love that the Christmas hours instill.

gifts
FOR ALL

Touch the special people in your life with Christmas gifts created especially for them. It'll be easy to please everyone with this great collection — and they'll never guess that your gifts were such bargains! For holiday chefs, you'll discover a cookie-decorating tree, machine appliquéd dish towels, and a handy recipe card holder set. Children will enjoy the Yuletide season with our angelic dress-up ensemble and crafty card-making kit. There are even fun creations such as our cute countdown chalkboard, stenciled throw rug, and painted stemware — all perfect for giving to teachers, neighbors, and party hostesses. You'll have your gift-giving all wrapped up with these wonderful ideas!

HOLIDAY RECIPE CARD SET

WHAT TO BUY

Photo album to hold 4" x 6"
    photos
$1/3$ yd fabric
$1^5/8$ yds $3/8$"w ribbon
Package of 100 4" x 6" index
    cards
Small cookie cutter

THINGS YOU HAVE AT HOME

Batting, glue, lightweight
cardboard, fusible web, and
pinking shears

TECHNIQUES YOU'LL NEED

Fusible Products (pg. 98)

*Whip up a batch of holiday fun with
our cute recipe holder and coordinating
recipe cards! A small photo album is
padded and dressed up with gingerbread-
motif fabric for the holder. To create
matching recipe cards, snippets of fabric
are fused to the corners of index cards. A
ribbon tie accented with a cookie cutter
organizes the cards in a neat bundle.*

RECIPE ALBUM AND CARDS

1. Measure width and height of open
album. Cut a piece of batting this size. Cut a
piece of fabric 2" larger on all sides than
batting.

2. Glue batting to outside of closed album.
Center open album on wrong side of fabric
piece. Glue corners of fabric over corners
of album. Glue edges of fabric over edges
of album, trimming to fit around hardware.

(Continued on pg. 40)

SWEET GINGERBREAD FRAME

WHAT TO BUY

Approx. 5¼"h gingerbread boy
   and girl cookie cutters
Tan felt piece
White baby rickrack
½ yd ⅛"w ribbon for bows
Two small jingle bells
2"w gold heart-shaped frame

THINGS YOU
HAVE AT HOME

Fusible web, poster board, glue,
2 small buttons, and small photo

TECHNIQUES
YOU'LL NEED

Fusible Products (pg. 98)

A sweet token for someone dear to your heart, this cookie-cutter couple holds a frame for displaying a favorite snapshot. The gingerbread boy and girl shapes are easily embellished with felt and rickrack "icing" trim.

GINGERBREAD PHOTO FRAME

1. Fuse felt to poster board. Draw around outside of each cookie cutter on poster board side of felt; cut out shapes just inside drawn lines. Glue shapes into cookie cutters.

2. Glue rickrack along edges of cookie cutters. Thread a 6" length of ribbon through hanger of jingle bell and tie into a bow; glue to gingerbread girl. Glue buttons to gingerbread boy.

3. Cut photo to fit in frame and secure in frame.

4. Thread remaining ribbon through hanger of remaining jingle bell and tie into a bow. Glue bow to top of frame. Glue loops of bow to gingerbread boy and girl.

FAUX STAINED GLASS GLOBE

WHAT TO BUY

11¹/₂"h hurricane globe
Package of red and green tissue
  paper
Silver dimensional paint
2 yds 1³/₈"w red velveteen ribbon
6¹/₂" dia. clay saucer
2⁷/₈" dia. x 6"h pillar candle

THINGS YOU HAVE AT HOME

Acetate, permanent felt-tip pen,
grease pencil, glue, red acrylic
paint, paintbrushes, paper towels,
floral wire, and wire cutters

TECHNIQUES YOU'LL NEED

Patterns (pg. 98)
Painting (pg. 100)
Multi-Loop Bows (pg. 102)

*S*hare the warmth of the holiday
season with this illuminating display.
Tissue paper cutouts and dimensional
paint create a stained glass look on the
hurricane globe, and a painted clay
saucer is used for the candle stand.
The holly-embellished gift is sure to
radiate your love.

YULETIDE GLOBE

1. Make patterns (pg. 40) from acetate.

2. Use grease pencil to draw around
patterns on globe.

3. Use patterns to cut the same number of
leaves and berries from tissue paper as
were drawn on globe.

4. Use paintbrush to apply glue to inside of
globe within drawn lines of 1 berry shape.

(Continued on pg. 40)

HOLIDAY TISSUE BOX COVER

Expect to Spend

tissue paper	1.19
tissue box cover	6.99
paint	.97
ribbon	.74
Total	**$9.89**

WHAT TO BUY

Green tissue paper
Wooden tissue box cover
Metallic gold acrylic paint
3/4 yd 5/8"w gold ribbon

THINGS YOU HAVE AT HOME

Foam brush, glue, motif cut from a Christmas card, small sponge piece, paper plate, paper towels, floral wire, and wire cutters

TECHNIQUES YOU'LL NEED

Painting (pg. 100)
Multi-Loop Bows (pg. 102)

This sponge-painted tissue box cover will add holiday dazzle to the vanity. Torn tissue paper provides rich texture to the wooden topper, which is finished with a Christmas card motif and a golden bow.

TISSUE BOX COVER

1. Tear tissue paper into small pieces. Use foam brush to apply glue to 1 area of box. Place tissue paper pieces over glue, forming wrinkles in paper with fingers and wrapping paper around edges of cover. Repeat to cover entire box.

2. Glue card motif to box.

3. Lightly sponge paint box gold.

4. Form ribbon into a multi-loop bow and glue to box.

YULETIDE TAPESTRY PILLOWS

WHAT TO BUY

¹/₂ yd fabric for each pillow
9" tapestry square for each pillow
One 8 oz. package polyester
    fiberfill for each pillow
Plaid Pillow:
²/₃ yd ¹/₄" dia. cord
4 skeins embroidery floss and a
    package of four ⁷/₈" long
    wooden beads for tassels
Ticking Pillow:
1²/₃ yds ⁵/₈"w ribbon
1²/₃ yds ⁷/₈"w ribbon for bows
Package of 4 jingle bells

THINGS YOU HAVE AT HOME

Fusible web and thread to match
fabric **Plaid Pillow:** Tapestry
needle and glue **Ticking Pillow:**
⁵/₈"w fusible web tape

TECHNIQUES YOU'LL NEED

Fusible Products (pg. 98)

*W*hether you need gifts with a whimsical touch or regal flair, our designer pillows are just the thing! Your friends will think you spent a fortune, but the pillows are inexpensive to fashion using ready-made tapestry squares, coordinating fabrics, and trims.

PLAID PILLOW

1. Cut two 15" fabric squares. Fuse web to wrong side of tapestry square. Center and fuse tapestry square to 1 fabric square (front).

2. Place fabric squares right sides together. Leaving an opening for turning, use a ¹/₂" seam allowance to sew squares together. Turn right side out and press. Stuff with fiberfill. Hand sew opening closed.

3. Beginning at 1 corner and knotting cord at each corner, glue cord along edges of tapestry square.

4. For each tassel, remove label from floss skein. Pull loose end of floss across skein and back to center (**Fig. 1**, pg. 40); wrap end twice around center of skein. Thread needle with end of floss and insert through bead, pushing bead close to skein. Fold skein over bead, smoothing floss and covering bead completely (**Fig. 2**, pg. 40).

(Continued on pg. 40)

CHRISTMAS TREE TOWELS

WHAT TO BUY

Approx. 18" x 28" red kitchen
  towel
¼ yd each of 2 green fabrics
Ecru felt piece
White baby rickrack

THINGS YOU
HAVE AT HOME

White thread and thread to match
fabrics and towel, tracing paper,
fabric marking pen, pinking
shears, glue, and buttons

TECHNIQUES
YOU'LL NEED

Patterns (pg. 98)

*Want an easy holiday gift that's
surprisingly inexpensive? Then try a pair
of our cheery tree-topped kitchen towels!
A plaid dish towel is cut in half, then
each half is finished with a padded
Christmas tree shape. Trimmed with
buttons, rickrack, and machine-stitched
"ornaments," the evergreen motifs will
provide a seasonal touch for the kitchen.*

CHRISTMAS TREE TOWELS

1. Wash, dry, and press towel and fabrics.

2. Match ends and fold towel in half; cut
along fold (raw edge is top of each towel
half).

3. Cut a 2½" x 44" strip from fabric for
hanging ties and set aside. Measure width
of towel half; add 3½". Cut a 1¼"w strip
from fabric the determined measurement
for tree trunk and towel trim. Press long
edges of 1¼"w strip to center on wrong
side. Cut a 3" length for tree trunk. Match
ends and press in half; stitching close to
pressed edges, sew side edges together. Set
trunk aside. For trim, press ends of
remaining part of strip ¼" to wrong side.
Sew trim about ⅜" from bottom edge of
towel.

(Continued on pg. 40)

FESTIVE CANDLE LIGHTS

WHAT TO BUY

Package of 2 battery-powered
candle lights
2 small self-adhesive lampshades
Fabric to cover lampshades
Trim to match fabric
1½ yds 1⅞"w wired ribbon for
bows
Metallic gold spray paint

THINGS YOU
HAVE AT HOME

Two 10¾-oz. soup cans,
corrugated cardboard, utility
knife, dried beans, masking tape,
and glue

*L*ight up Christmas with our festive
little lamp. A battery-powered candle
light is attached to a spray-painted can
for the base, and a mini lamp shade is
covered with pretty fabric to top it off.
A wired-ribbon bow adds a golden
glimmer. And because the lights
are sold in packs of two, why not
make an extra lamp for yourself
or to give to another friend!

CANDLE LIGHTS

1. Draw around 1 end of can on
cardboard. Use utility knife to cut out
circle. Fill can to just below rim with beans.
Glue circle just inside can opening (this
end is bottom of lamp base).

2. Glue base of light to unopened end of
can. Use tape to mask off candle and bulb.
Spray paint lamp base and can gold;
remove tape.

3. Cover shade with fabric. Glue trim to
shade.

4. Cut ribbon in half and tie 1 length into a
bow around lamp base; trim ends.

PICTURE-PERFECT BELLPULL

Finished in mere minutes, this beautiful bellpull will ring in the holidays with elegant style! The shimmering accent is fashioned from wired ribbon and trimmed with miniature frames displaying photos from Christmases past. Grandmother will adore this lovely gift!

WHAT TO BUY

1¹⁄₈ yds 2¹⁄₂"w wired ribbon
Tassel to match ribbon
Small photo frames

THINGS YOU HAVE AT HOME

8" of floral wire, photos to fit in frames, and glue

RIBBON BELLPULL

1. For backing, cut a 25" ribbon length. Fold ends ¹⁄₂" to wrong side and glue in place. For loop at top, fold 1 end 3" to wrong side and glue about ¹⁄₂" of end to back. Finger press a point at the other end (**Fig. 1**) and glue to secure. Glue hanger of tassel to back of point.

Fig. 1

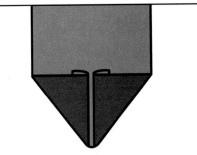

2. For bow, cut an 11" ribbon length for bow loops and a 1¹⁄₄" x 3" piece for bow center. Overlap ends of 11" length about ¹⁄₄" to form a loop; glue to secure. Flatten loop with overlap at center back and pinch at center to gather. Finger press long edges of bow center ribbon piece to center and wrap around loop; glue in place.

3. Wrap wire around loop at top of backing about 2³⁄₄" from top to gather. Glue bow over wire.

4. If necessary, remove easels from frames so frames will lie flat on backing. Place photos in frames. Glue frames to backing.

KEEPSAKE CHRISTMAS CARD

WHAT TO BUY

Wooden frame with backing to
hold card
4 colors of acrylic paint to match
card

THINGS YOU HAVE AT HOME

Christmas card and paintbrushes

TECHNIQUES YOU'LL NEED

Painting (pg. 100)

*I*nstead of stuffed in an envelope,
deliver your Christmas greeting card
first class — mounted inside a painted
wooden frame. Your sentiments can be
enjoyed as a decoration year after year!
This project is an even greater bargain
when you recycle garage-sale frames.

CUSTOM-FRAMED GREETING CARD

1. Use 2 colors of paint to paint wide
stripes on frame. Use additional paint
colors to paint lines on frame for plaid
design.

2. Secure card in frame.

PRETTY POINSETTIA COASTERS

WHAT TO BUY

Four 5" dia. 7-mesh hexagonal
   plastic canvas shapes
Needloft® yarn, 10 yd skeins:
   3 red (01)
   1 gold (17)
   1 green (27)
   3 white (41)
Basket with handle to hold
   coasters
Greenery pick

THINGS YOU HAVE AT HOME

Large tapestry needle, ribbons for
bow, and wire cutters (if needed)

TECHNIQUES YOU'LL NEED

Plastic Canvas Needlepoint
   (pg. 104)

*The spirit of Christmas blooms on
our colorful coasters featuring pretty
poinsettia motifs. Stitched on plastic
canvas shapes, these handy helpers work
up in no time. The coasters are sure to
spread holiday cheer when you deliver
them in a festive basket!*

POINSETTIA COASTER SET

1. Cut hangers from plastic canvas shapes.

2. Referring to chart and color key
(pg. 106), stitch design on each plastic
canvas shape. Use red yarn and Overcast
Stitch to finish edges of each shape.

3. If necessary, trim stem of greenery pick.
Tie ribbons into a bow around basket
handle; trim ends. Tuck pick behind bow.
Place coasters in basket.

17

ANGEL WALL QUILT

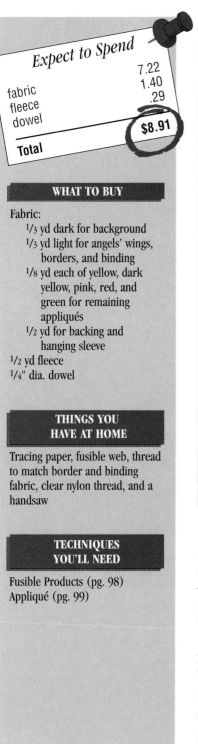
A gentle reminder of that holy night in Bethlehem, our heavenly wall hanging has the look of a little handmade quilt. However, this merry miniature is finished in no time using fused-on appliqués and machine quilting.

ANGEL WALL HANGING
Finished size: 16³/4" x 13¹/2"
1. Cut an 8¹/2" x 11³/4" piece from background fabric. Cut two 3" x 11³/4" strips for top and bottom borders and two 3" x 13¹/2" strips for side borders from border fabric.

2. (**Note:** Use a ¹/4" seam allowance unless otherwise indicated.) For wall hanging front, sew top and bottom borders to background fabric piece; press seam allowances toward background. Repeat to sew side borders to background.

3. Use patterns (pg. 107) to make appliqués. Arrange and fuse appliqués to wall hanging front.

4. Cut 1 piece each from fleece and backing fabric slightly larger than wall hanging front. Place fleece between wrong sides of wall hanging front and backing fabric piece; baste layers together.

(Continued on pg. 41)

STARRY NIGHT PILLOWCASE

WHAT TO BUY

White standard pillowcase
1/4 yd blue fabric for background
1/8 yd white flannel for snowdrift
    appliqués
2 1/3 yds 3/8"w red satin ribbon

THINGS YOU HAVE AT HOME

Fabric scraps for remaining
appliqués, fusible web, 3/8"w
fusible web tape, fusible tear-away
stabilizer, clear nylon and white
thread, black permanent felt-tip
pen, and a red colored pencil

TECHNIQUES YOU'LL NEED

Fusible Products (pg. 98)
Appliqué (pg. 99)

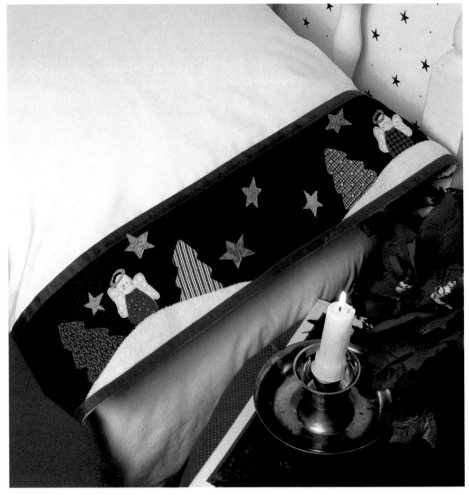

This angel-embellished pillowcase will brighten up the bedroom! A simple starry night scene is created from machine appliquéd fabric cutouts.

ANGELS AND STARS PILLOWCASE

1. Wash, dry, and press pillowcase, fabrics, and ribbon.

2. Fuse web to wrong side of blue fabric. Measure around pillowcase opening; add 1/2". Cut a 4 1/4"w fabric strip the determined length (if pillowcase hem width is more than 4 1/4", cut a fabric strip same width as hem by determined length). Cut 2 ribbon lengths same length as fabric strip.

3. Overlapping ends at seam, fuse fabric strip about 1/4" from opening of pillowcase.

4. Use patterns (pg. 107) to make appliqués. Arrange appliqués on fabric strip and fuse in place. Use clear thread to stitch appliqués in place.

5. Fuse web tape to ribbon lengths. Overlapping ends at seam, fuse ribbon lengths over edges of fabric strip. Use a straight stitch to stitch along edges of ribbon lengths.

6. Use pen to draw eyes on angels and colored pencil to color cheeks.

EXQUISITE VANITY SET

Expect to Spend

bottle	1.29
fabric	1.46
cord	.68
ribbon	.70
roses	1.99
mirror trivet	2.97

Total $9.09

WHAT TO BUY

Glass vanity bottle with stopper
1/3 yd sheer fabric
Fine gold cord
1/3 yd 1 1/2"w wired ribbon for
  bow
Gold ribbon roses (we used 11)
Mirror trivet

THINGS YOU HAVE AT HOME

Rubber band and glue

*D*elight a friend who loves feminine accents with our exquisite vanity set. The lavish pairing includes a glass decanter embellished with sheer fabric and gilded trims and a decorated mirror for displaying the beautiful bottle.

VANITY BOTTLE WITH MIRROR TRAY
1. Measure bottle from top around widest point of bottom and back up to top. Cut a circle of fabric this diameter. Center bottle on wrong side of fabric. Wrap fabric up around bottle and hold in place at neck of bottle with rubber band. Tuck raw edges to wrong side just below top of bottle and secure under rubber band; glue to secure and remove rubber band.

2. Knot a length of cord around neck of bottle and fabric; trim ends. Tie ribbon into a bow and glue to bottle over knot in cord. Glue roses to bow. Wrap and glue cord around sides and top of stopper. Glue rose to stopper.

3. Glue a length of cord along edge of trivet. Glue roses to cord, covering ends.

ELEGANT CHRISTMAS ALBUM

WHAT TO BUY

Photo album
1/2 yd fabric
1 5/8 yds 7/8"w ribbon
Silk poinsettias and holly sprigs

THINGS YOU HAVE AT HOME

Batting, glue, lightweight cardboard, floral wire, and wire cutters

TECHNIQUES YOU'LL NEED

Multi-Loop Bows (pg. 102)

The perfect place to store Christmas memories, this elegantly decorated photo album will be a cherished gift. Gilded ribbon and silk holly and poinsettia sprigs decorate the front of the festive fabric-covered holder.

COVERED CHRISTMAS ALBUM

1. Measure width and height of open album. Cut a piece of batting this size. Cut a piece of fabric 2" larger on all sides than batting.

2. Glue batting to outside of closed album. Center open album on wrong side of fabric piece. Glue corners of fabric over corners of album. Glue edges of fabric over edges of album, trimming to fit around hardware.

(Continued on pg. 41)

ANGEL DRESS-UP SET

*T*his adorable dress-up ensemble is a young girl's dream! The set includes a star-tipped wand, a wispy skirt, wings, and a halo — all tucked inside a heavenly gift bag for your favorite little angel.

WHAT TO BUY

1³/8 yds 45"w white netting
Spool of gold curling ribbon
Gold star garland
1½ yd package ½"w elastic
White feather boa
Balloon stick
Large white gift bag

THINGS YOU HAVE AT HOME

Large needle, glue, tracing paper, poster board, and a gold paint pen

TECHNIQUES YOU'LL NEED

Patterns (pg. 98)
Embroidery (pg. 103)

Fig. 1

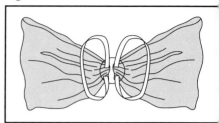

ANGEL DRESS-UP KIT

Note: We made our skirt and wings to fit a toddler. Adjust measurements as needed to fit your child.

1. For skirt, cut a 23" x 1³/8 yd piece of netting. Fold netting in half lengthwise. Thread needle with a 1½ yd length of curling ribbon. Leaving about 18" of ribbon at each end, work a Running Stitch about ½" from fold of skirt. Push netting toward center of ribbon to gather skirt and knot ribbon at each side of netting; adjust gathers evenly. Curl ribbon ends. Cut stars from garland and glue to skirt.

2. For wing base, make circle pattern (pg. 108). Use pattern to cut two circles from poster board. For each wing, cut a 20" x 22" piece of netting. Fold long edges 2" to 1 side (wrong side). Matching wrong sides and short edges, fold in half. Gather short edges tightly and glue to 1 poster board circle (**Fig. 1**). For shoulder straps, cut two 20" lengths of elastic. Glue ends of elastic lengths to poster board circle (**Fig. 1**). Glue remaining poster board circle over ends of wings and straps. Cut one 7" length and two 18" lengths from boa. Glue short length over poster board circle on side of wings opposite straps. Glue 1 long length along outer edge of each wing. Cut several stars from garland and glue to wings.

3. For halo, wind a 6 ft. length of star garland into an approx. 7" dia. circle; wrap ends around garland circle to secure. Wrap remaining boa length around garland circle, tucking ends through garland circle to secure. Tie lengths of curling ribbon around halo and curl ends.

4. For wand, cut a small square of netting. Tightly gather 1 edge between fingers and glue to secure. Form a length of garland into a star shape with a 3" tail. Wrap tail of star around gathered edge of netting. Glue tail of star into top of balloon stick. Tie lengths of curling ribbon to top of balloon stick and curl.

5. Use paint pen to write "for an Angel" and paint stars on bag. Tie lengths of curling ribbon around bag handle and curl.

for an Angel

SANTA COUNTDOWN

WHAT TO BUY

Approx. 7$\frac{1}{2}$" x 9$\frac{1}{2}$" wood-framed chalkboard

White, red, brown, and black craft foam

$\frac{3}{4}$"h white self-stick letters

1$\frac{1}{8}$ yds ribbon about same width as frame to cover frame

1$\frac{2}{3}$ yds narrow red and 1$\frac{1}{3}$ yds narrow white ribbon for bow

THINGS YOU HAVE AT HOME

Tracing paper, cosmetic powder, craft stick, black felt-tip pen, a piece of chalk, and glue

TECHNIQUES YOU'LL NEED

Patterns (pg. 98)
Multi-Loop Bows (pg. 102)

A teacher will love displaying this playful sign to remind students of how soon Santa will be coming! To make the sign, a mini chalkboard is dressed up with ribbons, a craft-foam Santa, and self-stick letters. To spread the fun around, the teacher can choose a different student each day to update the Christmas countdown.

CHRISTMAS COUNTDOWN BOARD

1. Overlapping ribbon at corners and wrapping ends to back, glue ribbon lengths over chalkboard frame.

2. Make Santa and sack patterns (pgs. 108 and 109). Use patterns to cut shapes from foam.

3. Use fingertip to shade face with powder.

(Continued on pg. 41)

SNAZZY SNOWMAN WREATH

WHAT TO BUY

Small grapevine wreath
White felt piece
Fabric:
 $1/4$ yd white
 $1/8$ yd green
 $1/4$ yd red for bow
Three $2^1/2$"w wooden snowflake
 cutouts
White acrylic paint

THINGS YOU HAVE AT HOME

Fabric scraps for remaining
appliqués, fusible web,
paintbrushes, buttons, thread,
black felt-tip pen, and glue

TECHNIQUES YOU'LL NEED

Fusible Products (pg. 98)
Appliqué (pg. 99)

A snazzy dresser, our frosty felt fellow adds wintry appeal to a grapevine wreath. Buttons, torn fabric strips, wooden snowflakes, and a checked flannel bow also deck the winsome wall accent.

SNOWMAN WREATH

1. For snowman, fuse a 9" x 12" piece of white fabric to 1 side of felt. Use patterns (pg. 109) to make appliqués. Arrange and fuse appliqués to remaining side of felt. Cut out snowman.

2. Paint white highlights in eyes. Use pen to draw mouth. Paint snowflake cutouts white.

3. Tear green fabric into $1/2$"w strips. For scarf, tear an 8" length from 1 strip and tie around neck. Sew buttons to vest.

4. For bow, press fabric piece in half lengthwise with right side out. Fuse wrong sides together. Cut a $2^1/4$"w strip from fabric. Tie into a bow.

5. Wrap remaining green fabric strips around wreath and glue to secure. Glue snowman, snowflakes, bow, and buttons to wreath.

"HOLLY-DAYS" STEMWARE

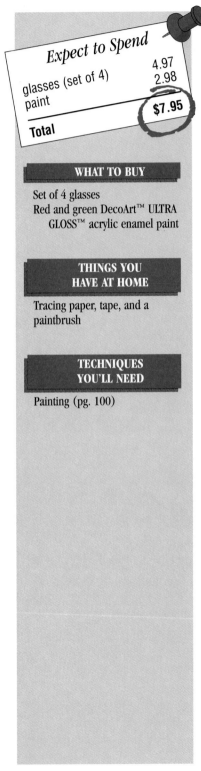

Expect to Spend

glasses (set of 4)	4.97
paint	2.98
Total	**$7.95**

WHAT TO BUY

Set of 4 glasses
Red and green DecoArt™ ULTRA
GLOSS™ acrylic enamel paint

THINGS YOU HAVE AT HOME

Tracing paper, tape, and a paintbrush

TECHNIQUES YOU'LL NEED

Painting (pg. 100)

*F*riends and neighbors will toast the holidays — and you — with your festive gift of hand-painted stemware! The simple holly pattern is super easy to apply, so a set of four can be finished in a flash.

PAINTED STEMWARE

1. (**Note:** We recommend hand washing glasses after use.) Trace pattern (pg. 109) onto tracing paper; leaving a little room around design, cut out pattern. Tape pattern inside glass.

2. Use pattern as a guide to paint leaves and berries on glass. On bottom of glass, paint straight and wavy lines from center out. Paint dots between lines.

3. Follow manufacturer's instructions to cure paint.

CHEERY TABLE RUNNER

WHAT TO BUY

Fabric:
- ¹/₂ yd of 60"w for table runner
- ¹/₄ yd brown for reindeer
- ¹/₈ yd red for Santa's hat and coat
- ¹/₄ yd green for tree

White felt piece for Santa's hat trim, beard, and mustache

²/₃ yd 1"w red grosgrain ribbon

¹/₂ yd ¹/₄"w ribbon for bows

2 large jingle bells

THINGS YOU HAVE AT HOME

1"w fusible web tape, fabric scraps for Santa's face and mitten appliqués, fusible web, tracing paper, transfer paper, stylus, black permanent felt-tip pen, red colored pencil, fusible tear-away stabilizer, clear nylon thread, sewing thread to match runner fabric, glue, buttons, and 2 safety pins

TECHNIQUES YOU'LL NEED

Patterns (pg. 98)
Fusible Products (pg. 98)
Appliqué (pg. 99)

*S*pread a little Christmas cheer with this terrific table runner! Jingle bell and button accents make the housewarming token even merrier.

CHRISTMAS TABLE RUNNER

1. Wash, dry, and press fabric, felt, and ribbon.

2. Cut a point at each end of runner fabric piece (**Fig. 1**).

Fig. 1

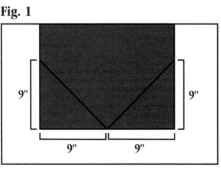

3. Use web tape to hem long edges, then short edges of fabric piece.

4. Use all patterns except antler and Santa's eye patterns (pgs. 110 and 111) to make appliqués. For ribbon appliqués, fuse web tape to 1"w ribbon. Cut ribbon in half.

5. Arrange appliqués at ends of runner; fuse in place.

6. Transfer antler and Santa's eye patterns (pg. 110) to runner. Use pen to color antlers and eyes. Use pencil to color Santa's cheeks.

7. Use clear thread to stitch appliqués in place.

8. Glue buttons to runner for noses, ornaments, and reindeer's eyes. Cut ¹/₄"w ribbon in half. Thread 1 length through hanger on each bell and tie into a bow. Use safety pins on wrong side of runner to pin bells to points.

SANTA BEAR

Expect to Spend

bear	2.99
fur	2.00
felt	.20
ribbon	.50
sock (2 pack)	1.50
bells (4 pack)	.69
glasses	.86
tree	.99
Total	**$9.73**

WHAT TO BUY

12"h jointed teddy bear
1/4 yd white artificial fur
Black felt piece for boots
1/2 yd 1/2"w ribbon for boots
Adult red slouch-style sock for hat
3 jingle bells
Wire doll glasses to fit bear (ours
    measure 3 1/2"w)
6"h artificial Christmas tree

THINGS YOU
HAVE AT HOME

Tracing paper, small sharp
scissors, glue, cosmetic blush, red
and black thread, polyester
fiberfill, poster board for tag, red
felt-tip pen, hole punch, and red
embroidery floss

TECHNIQUES
YOU'LL NEED

Patterns (pg. 98)

This sweet Santa is really a teddy bear in disguise. Who could resist the cheery charms of this adorable little fellow dressed up in a furry white beard, hat, and glasses!

SANTA BEAR

1. Make eyebrow and beard patterns (pg. 112). Use patterns to cut eyebrows and beard from fur, cutting through backing of fur only. Cut an approx. 1" x 14 1/2" fur strip for hat trim. Trim fur on eyebrows short.

2. Glue eyebrows to bear. Apply blush to cheeks.

3. For hat, cut ribbed tube section from sock; discard toe. Turn tube wrong side out. For top, baste along raw edge of tube. Pull threads to close end; knot threads.

Turn hat right side out. Sew bell to top. Place hat on bear. Place beard on bear and tack top corners inside hat. Glue hat trim along bottom edge of hat. Fold top of hat to 1 side and glue in place. Place glasses on bear.

4. For boots, make pattern (pg. 112). For each boot, use pattern to cut boot from felt. Fold boot along fold line. Use a 1/4" seam allowance to sew front and bottom edges. Turn right side out and stuff toe with fiberfill. Sew bell to toe. Place boot on foot and fold top edge about 1/2" to inside; cut ribbon in half and knot 1 length around top.

5. For tag on tree, cut tag shape from poster board. Use pen to write greeting. Punch a hole in tag. Use floss to tie tag to tree. Place tree under arm of bear.

KIDS' CHRISTMAS CARD KIT

WHAT TO BUY

Construction paper tablet
1/3 yd fabric
Package of 8 markers
3/4 yd 7/8"w ribbon
Box of 24 crayons
Craft glue stick
Children's craft scissors

THINGS YOU HAVE AT HOME

Fusible web, thread to match fabric, pinking shears, cotton string, and a rubber band

TECHNIQUES YOU'LL NEED

Fusible Products (pg. 98)

Children enjoy creating things for others, and they'll love receiving their very own Christmas card-making kit! A drawstring bag made from holiday fabric holds markers, crayons, a glue stick, and scissors. The goody bag is presented with a fabric-covered tablet of construction paper so youngsters can begin crafting holiday greetings right away!

CHRISTMAS CARD-MAKING KIT

1. Fuse web to wrong side of fabric to cover tablet. Cut a piece of fabric slightly smaller than front of tablet. Center and fuse fabric to tablet.

2. For bag, cut a 7" x 22" fabric piece. Matching right sides and short edges, fold fabric in half (fold is bottom of bag). Using a 1/2" seam allowance, sew sides of bag together. Turn right side out. Use pinking shears to trim top.

3. For drawstring, cut a 28" length of string. Pin string around bag 1 1/2" from top with ends at right side. Beginning at right side of bag, use a wide zigzag stitch with a long stitch length to sew over string, being careful not to catch string in stitching.

4. Wrap rubber band around markers. Tie ribbon into a bow over rubber band; trim ends. Place markers, crayons, glue stick, and scissors in bag.

CHRISTMAS GROWTH CHART

Expect to Spend

fabric	1.00
tape measure	.94
ribbon	.50
paint	.97
stencils	3.95
dowel	.39
beads	1.09
	$8.84
Total	

*H*elp a growing family start
a new Christmas tradition with our
holly-jolly growth chart! Every Yuletide,
little ones' names and the year can be
added in permanent marker next to the
appropriate height. A lasting keepsake
that parents will treasure, the chart is
simply fashioned from a piece of
fabric with a tape measure sewn to
one side. With a stenciled message
and cheery painted motifs, this gift
is sure to measure up!

SANTA GROWTH CHART

1. For chart, cut a 10" x 50" piece from
fabric. Make a ³/₈" hem in each edge. Make
a 1" casing at 1 end (top).

2. Cut tape measure just below the 20"
mark and trim metal end from the other
end. Pin tape measure about ¹/₂" from right
and bottom edges of chart. Sew tape
measure to chart.

3. Transfer Santa pattern (pgs. 114
and 115) to top of chart and ribbon end
pattern (pg. 115) to bottom of chart.

4. To draw the rest of the ribbon, use fabric
marking pencil to draw 1 wavy line between
the two parts of the design (red line in
Diagram) and another wavy line
intersecting the first one (blue line in
Diagram).

5. Use fabric marking pencil and lettering
stencils to draw letters to spell "SANTA
WATCH ME GROW" next to the ribbon.

6. Basecoat Santa's hat and sleeves red.
Leaving a little white showing for highlights
paint nose and ribbon red. Drybrush
centers of bricks red. Paint face peach. Mix
a little red and peach paint together to
paint cheeks. Paint eyes, gloves, and letters
black. Paint black checks along edges of
chart.

7. Use black pen to outline designs.

8. Cut dowel to 10¹/₄". Place dowel in
casing and glue beads to ends. Knot ends o
a 22" ribbon length around ends of dowel.
Form remaining ribbon into a multi-loop
bow tied with ribbon at center and glue to
chart.

9. Hang chart so that 20" mark is 20" from
floor.

DIAGRAM

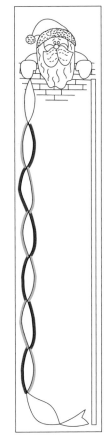

31

TICK-TOCK ELF CLOCK

Expect to Spend

clock	4.99
fabric	1.85
ribbon	.42
bell (4 pack)	.69
Total	**$7.95**

WHAT TO BUY

6¹/₂" dia. battery-powered
   clock
Fabric:
   ¹/₄ yd muslin
   ¹/₈ yd red print
   ¹/₈ yd red stripe
   ¹/₈ yd green print
¹/₄ yd each of 3 ribbons for bow
Jingle bell

THINGS YOU HAVE AT HOME

Fusible web, poster board, tracing paper, transfer paper, stylus, black felt-tip pen, cosmetic blush, ruler, yarn for hair, 2 small buttons, and glue

TECHNIQUES YOU'LL NEED

Patterns (pg. 98)
Fusible Products (pg. 98)
Appliqué (pg. 99)

Our elfish timekeeper is a playful present for folks who like to stay on schedule during the holidays! Fabric cutouts fused to poster board are glued to the back of the clock to form the mischievous fellow. A jingle bell and bow trim his hat, and buttons accent his shoes. Santa's little helper is a terrific reminder that time is ticking away for making all those special gifts.

ELF CLOCK

1. Use head, hat, hand, legs, and feet patterns (pg. 113) to make appliqués. Fuse shapes separately to poster board; cut out shapes.

2. Transfer face pattern (pg. 113) to head. Use pen to draw over face and color eyes. Use fingertip to shade cheeks with blush.

3. Use pen and ruler to draw lines at centers of legs and feet.

4. For hair, cut four lengths of yarn. Extending yarn above head, glue yarn to back of head. Thread ribbons through hanger on bell and tie into a bow; glue to hat. Glue buttons to feet.

5. Glue head to hat and feet to legs. Glue head and legs to back of clock. Glue hand to opposite sides of clock.

STENCILED FLOOR COVER

Expect to Spend

rug	4.99
paint	2.91
embroidery floss	.40
yarn	.87
Total	**$9.17**

WHAT TO BUY

21" x 35" cotton rug with fringe
Red, green, and brown acrylic
 paint
Red and green embroidery floss
Red yarn

THINGS YOU
HAVE AT HOME

Yardstick, acetate, permanent felt-
tip pen, craft knife, cutting mat,
stencil brush, paper plates, paper
towels, and a tapestry needle

TECHNIQUES
YOU'LL NEED

Painting (pg. 100)
Embroidery (pg. 103)

*This stenciled floor cover is just
the thing to add Christmas charm to a
kitchen or entry hall. The quilt-look pine
tree and nine-patch motifs are painted
onto a plain throw rug and enhanced
with straight stitches.*

STENCILED RUG

1. For guidelines, use yardstick and a
pencil to lightly draw eight 6" squares at
center of rug. For checkerboard squares,
divide 4 of the squares into nine 2"
squares.

2. Use tree, tree trunk, and checkerboard
patterns (pg. 115) to make stencils.

3. Aligning squares in checkerboard stencil
with squares drawn on rug, stencil green
checks on rug. Stencil alternating checks
red. Stencil green trees and brown tree
trunks in remaining squares.

4. Use red floss to work Running Stitch
around trees. Use green floss to work
Running Stitch along edges of squares with
trees.

5. Knot yarn lengths around alternating
fringe sections on rug. Trim ends even with
fringe and fray.

POINSETTIA TOPIARY

WHAT TO BUY

4"h clay pot
Metallic gold acrylic paint
Poinsettia bush with about 10
   flowers
2 gold pinecone picks
   (3 pinecones per pick)
Three 12" long cinnamon sticks
Two 3" x 4" x 8" floral foam
   bricks
1 yd 2½"w wired ribbon

THINGS YOU
HAVE AT HOME

Ivory acrylic paint, foam brush,
small sponge piece, paper plates,
paper towels, glue, serrated knife,
floral wire, wire cutters, and
Spanish moss

TECHNIQUES
YOU'LL NEED

Painting (pg. 100)

*A terrific way to trim the table,
our timeless topiary is easy to make
— and even nicer to give. To create
the centerpiece, we simply glued faux
poinsettias and pinecones to floral foam.*

POINSETTIA TOPIARY

1. Use foam brush to apply ivory basecoat
to pot. Sponge paint pot gold.

2. Cut about 3" from 1 end of each foam
brick. Fill pot with 3" foam pieces to about
1" from rim; glue to secure. For top of
topiary, glue 4" x 5" surfaces of remaining
foam pieces together. Use knife to round off
corners of foam.

3. For trunk, wire cinnamon sticks togeth
at each end. Insert 1 end of trunk about 3
into foam in pot and remaining end into
top; glue to secure. Glue moss over top an
foam in pot.

4. Leaving 2" stems on flowers, cut
poinsettias from bush; insert stems into to
of topiary. Remove pinecones from picks
and some leaves from poinsettia bush.
Wrap a wire length around each leaf stem
and large end of each pinecone; insert int
top of topiary and foam in pot.

5. Glue a length of ribbon around rim of
pot. Tie remaining ribbon into a bow. Wra
a length of wire around back of bow and
insert ends into pot.

FESTIVE PHOTO MAT

WHAT TO BUY

Pre-cut mat with 3" wide borders
   (our 11" x 14" mat holds two
   3" x 4½" photos)
⅝ yd 1½"w ribbon for bow

THINGS YOU
HAVE AT HOME

Tracing paper, transfer paper,
stylus, colored pencils, black felt-
tip pen, photo(s) or Christmas
card(s) to fit in mat, tape, poster
board, 4" of floral wire for
hanger, and glue

TECHNIQUES
YOU'LL NEED

Patterns (pg. 98)

*H*and-shaded holly vines elegantly
frame a merry sentiment and a snapshot
on our lovely photo mat frame. A festive
bow completes the gift.

HOLLY FRAME

1. Transfer holly pattern (pg. 116) to mat.

2. Use pencils to color and shade design.
Use black pen to draw over lines of design.

3. To frame photo or card, draw around
mat opening on photo or card and cut out
shape about ½" outside drawn shape. Tape
photo or card to back of mat.

4. Draw around mat on poster board; cut
out shape and glue to back of mat.

5. For hanger, bend wire ends slightly.
Center wire across back of mat about 2"
from top; glue ends in place.

6. Tie ribbon into a bow and glue to mat.

BREAD WARMER BASKET

WHAT TO BUY

Fabric:
   ¹/₄ yd for background
   ¹/₄ yd green for wreath
   ¹/₃ yd red for bow and
      basket liner
¹/₄ yd cotton fleece
6" square unglazed terra-cotta tile
Basket

THINGS YOU HAVE AT HOME

Fusible interfacing, fusible web, tracing paper, transfer paper, stylus, fusible tear-away stabilizer, thread to match fabrics, and pinking shears

TECHNIQUES YOU'LL NEED

Patterns (pg. 98)
Fusible Products (pg. 98)
Appliqué (pg. 99)

*L*ift a neighbor's spirits with our merry bread warmer and lined basket. An appliquéd wreath decorates the warmer, which includes a pocket to hold a heated tile. Leftover fabric is fringed for the basket liner.

HOLIDAY BREAD WARMER

1. Cut two 8" squares and one 8" x 12¹/₂" piece from background fabric. Cut an 8" square from fleece.

2. Fuse interfacing to wrong side of one fabric square (top).

3. Use patterns (pg. 118) to make appliqués. Fuse appliqués to top.

4. Transfer detail lines of bow pattern to bow.

5. Stitch appliqués in place. Stitch along detail lines on bow.

6. To assemble warmer, place fleece squar[e] between wrong sides of fabric squares. Fo[r] pocket, match wrong sides and short edge[s] and press 8" x 12¹/₂" fabric piece in half. Match raw edges of pocket to side and bottom edges on back of layered squares.

(Continued on pg. 4[1]

"BABY'S FIRST" ALBUM

WHAT TO BUY

12¹/₄"w x 14¹/₄"h scrapbook
Fabric:
  ¹/₂ yd green for background
  ¹/₃ yd red plaid for trim
  ¹/₄ yd brown for pony

THINGS YOU HAVE AT HOME

Fusible web, fabric scraps for remaining appliqués, glue, small buttons, tracing paper, transfer paper, stylus, and string or yarn

TECHNIQUES YOU'LL NEED

Patterns (pg. 98)
Fusible Products (pg. 98)
Appliqué (pg. 99)

A gift that new parents will cherish, our "baby's first" Christmas album is decorated with fused-on fabric appliqués. String spells out the precious title.

"BABY'S FIRST" ALBUM

1. Fuse web to wrong sides of fabrics for background and trim. Cut a piece from background fabric slightly smaller than front of scrapbook; center and fuse to scrapbook. Cut a 1"w strip from trim fabric same length as each edge of scrapbook. Fuse strips along edges of scrapbook front.

2. Use patterns (pg. 117) to make appliqués. Arrange and fuse appliqués to scrapbook.

3. Glue buttons to scrapbook for pony's eye and center of each wheel. Thread 1 end of a length of string through a button and knot end; knot remaining end. Glue to scrapbook for pull.

4. Transfer "baby's first" pattern (pg. 116) to scrapbook. Draw over words with a thin line of glue. Lay lengths of string over glue.

COOKIE LOVER'S TREE

WHAT TO BUY

Small artificial evergreen tree
3 cookie cutters
Package of 6 containers of
    decorating sprinkles
Tube of decorating gel
2 wooden spoons
Christmas pot holder

THINGS YOU
HAVE AT HOME

Floral wire and either string or
yarn

*D*elight a cookie connoisseur with a
miniature tree adorned with everything
needed to decorate home-baked treats! A
cheery pot holder is the tree skirt, and for
the tree-topper, there's a star-shaped
cookie cutter.

COOKIE DECORATING KIT
1. Use lengths of string to tie cookie cutter
and sprinkle containers to tree. Wire
decorating gel tube and spoons between
branches.

2. Place tree on pot holder.

38

Expect to Spend

fabric	4.65
embroidery floss	.20
greenery sprig	1.27
Total	**$6.12**

WHAT TO BUY

Fabric:
- 1/3 yd for stocking
- 1/3 yd for lining
- 1/4 yd of 1 fabric and 1/8 yd each of 3 additional fabrics for panel

Skein of embroidery floss
Greenery sprig

THINGS YOU HAVE AT HOME

Fusible web, tracing paper, fabric marking pencil, fabric scraps for appliqués and hanger, tapestry needle, thread to match fabrics, glue, and buttons

TECHNIQUES YOU'LL NEED

Patterns (pg. 98)
Fusible Products (pg. 98)
Appliqué (pg. 99)
Embroidery (pg. 103)

*F*estive fabrics give this simple stocking homespun appeal. Decked with buttons and fused-on appliqués, the country charmer will delight anyone who has a love for old-fashioned trimmings.

COUNTRY STOCKING

1. Cut two 10" x 16" fabric pieces each for stocking and lining.

2. Fuse web to fabrics for panel. Cut 10" long strips the following widths: 5³/₄", 1³/₄", 1³/₈", and 1". Arrange and fuse strips to 1 stocking fabric piece (front) in the order shown in **Diagram**, pg. 41.

3. Pin stocking fabric pieces right sides together. Make stocking pattern (pg. 119). Center pattern on fabric pieces with top of pattern even with 1 end (top) of fabric

(Continued on pg. 41)

HOLIDAY RECIPE CARD SET
(Continued from pg. 8)

3. For ties, cut two 10" lengths of ribbon. Glue end of 1 ribbon length inside front and back cover of album.

4. Cut two 2"w fabric strips same length as height of album. Press ends $1/2$" to wrong side. Center and glue 1 strip along each side of binding hardware with 1 long edge tucked under hardware. Cut 2 cardboard pieces $1/2$" smaller on all sides than album front. Cut 2 fabric pieces 1" larger on all sides than 1 cardboard piece. Center 1 cardboard piece on wrong side of 1 fabric piece. Glue corners of fabric over corners of cardboard. Glue edges of fabric over edges of cardboard. Repeat to cover remaining cardboard piece. Glue covered cardboard pieces inside front and back of album.

5. Close album and tie ribbons into a bow.

6. For recipe cards, fuse web to wrong side of fabric. Use pinking shears to cut motifs from fabric. Fuse a motif to corner of each index card. Tie remaining ribbon into a bow around cards and cookie cutter.

FAUX STAINED GLASS GLOBE
(Continued from pg. 10)

Place a tissue paper berry over glue and smooth in place. Repeat for remaining berries and leaves. Use a damp paper towel to remove any excess glue.

5. Use a paper towel to remove grease pencil from globe. Painting on outside of globe, use silver paint to paint veins on leaves and outline leaves and berries.

6. Cut ribbon in half. Form 1 ribbon length into a multi-loop bow. Tie remaining length around bottom of globe. Knot ribbon ends around bow; trim ends.

7. Paint red basecoat on saucer. Place candle on inverted saucer. Place globe over candle.

YULETIDE TAPESTRY PILLOWS
(Continued from pg. 12)

Tightly wrap end of floss twice around skein at bottom of bead; use needle to knot floss. Push needle back up through bead. Stitch tassel to corner of pillow and pass needle back through bead. Knot and trim end of floss at center of tassel below bead. Cut floss loops and trim tassel ends even.

Fig. 1

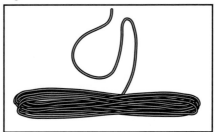

Fig. 2

TICKING PILLOW
1. Follow Step 1 of Plaid Pillow instructions, pg. 12.

2. Fuse web tape to wrong side of $5/8$"w ribbon. Cut ribbon into four 15" lengths. Arrange lengths on pillow front, covering edges of tapestry square, and fuse in place.

3. Follow Step 2 of Plaid Pillow instructions.

4. Cut $7/8$"w ribbon into four 15" lengths. Tie each length into a bow. Sew 1 bow and 1 bell to pillow at each corner of tapestry square.

CHRISTMAS TREE TOWELS
(Continued from pg. 13)

4. Cut two 6" x 7" pieces from fabric and one 6" x 7" piece from felt. Place felt piece between wrong sides of fabric pieces. Make tree pattern (pg. 106). Use fabric marking pencil to draw around pattern on fabric. Leaving bottom edge open, sew layers together along drawn line. Use pinking shears to trim seam allowance to about $1/4$" and bottom of tree to about $1/4$" from drawn line.

5. Press pleats in top of towel half (**Fig. 1**).

Fig. 1

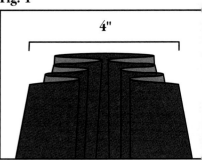

6. Insert raw end of trunk under felt at center bottom of tree; glue to felt to secure. With trunk at front, insert top of towel half into opening at bottom of tree. Stitch along drawn line at bottom of tree to secure towel in tree.

7. Sew rickrack to tree for decoration and along trim at bottom of towel. For ornaments, use a wide zigzag stitch with a very short stitch length to sew blocks of stitches on tree. Sew buttons to tree.

8. For hanging ties, press ends of $2^1/2$"w fabric strip $1/4$" to wrong side. Matching wrong sides, press strip in half lengthwise; unfold. Press long edges to center; refold. Stitch close to pressed edges. Match ends and fold strip in half; sew fold to top back of tree.

ANGEL WALL QUILT
(Continued from pg. 18)

Use clear thread to stitch "in the ditch" (close to seamlines) along inner edges of borders. Trim backing and fleece even with edges of wall hanging front.

For hanging sleeve, cut a 3" x 15½" fabric strip; sew a ¼" hem in each short edge. Matching wrong sides, press hanging sleeve in half lengthwise. Match raw edges of hanging sleeve to center top edge of backing; baste in place. Hand stitch bottom of hanging sleeve to backing.

For binding, cut a 1⅝" x 2 yd fabric strip, piecing as necessary. Press 1 end ¼" to wrong side. Matching wrong sides, press strip in half lengthwise; unfold. Press long edges to center; refold strip.

To attach binding to wall hanging, unfold 1 long edge of binding. Beginning with pressed end of binding at least 3" from a corner and matching right side of binding to wall hanging front, pin unfolded edge of binding along edges of wall hanging. Using pressing line closest to raw edge as a guide, sew binding to wall hanging, mitering binding at corners, until ends of binding overlap ½"; trim excess binding. Fold binding over raw edges to back of wall hanging; hand stitch in place. Remove basting threads.

Cut dowel to 15½". Place dowel in sleeve.

ELEGANT CHRISTMAS ALBUM
(Continued from pg. 21)

Cut a ribbon length 4" longer than height of album. Glue ribbon to album front, folding ends to inside.

Cut two 2"w fabric strips same length as height of album. Press ends ½" to wrong side. Center and glue 1 strip along each side of binding hardware with 1 long edge tucked under hardware. Cut 2

cardboard pieces ½" smaller on all sides than album front. Cut 2 fabric pieces 1" larger on all sides than 1 cardboard piece. Center 1 cardboard piece on wrong side of 1 fabric piece. Glue corners of fabric over corners of cardboard. Glue edges of fabric over edges of cardboard. Repeat to cover remaining cardboard piece. Glue covered cardboard pieces inside front and back of album.

5. Form a multi-loop bow from remaining ribbon. Glue poinsettias, holly, and bow to album.

SANTA COUNTDOWN
(Continued from pg. 24)

4. Glue Santa pieces together. Use pen to draw eyes on Santa. With arms and sack overlapping front of chalkboard and bottom edge of Santa at back, glue Santa to chalkboard. Glue craft stick to back of Santa and chalkboard for support.

5. Arrange self-stick letters on chalkboard to spell "Santa comes in ___ days" (use 3 "I's" placed end to end for blank line and asterisks for snowflakes).

6. For bow, cut a 12" length of red ribbon. Form a multi-loop bow from remaining ribbons and tie at center with 1 end of the 12" ribbon length. Knot the other end of the 12" ribbon length around chalk piece. Glue bow to chalkboard.

BREAD WARMER BASKET
(Continued from pg. 36)

Pin all layers together. Sew about ⅝" from raw edges. Use pinking shears to trim edges of warmer. Place tile in warmer.

7. Cut a piece from remaining fabric to line basket; fringe edges. Place liner and warmer in basket. Give with instructions for using warmer: Preheat oven to 350 degrees. Remove tile from warmer and place in oven for 15 minutes. Use tongs to return tile to warmer. Place warmer in basket.

COUNTRY STOCKING
(Continued from pg. 39)

pieces; use fabric marking pencil to draw around pattern. Cut out stocking pieces ½" outside drawn lines. Repeat for lining.

4. Use tree, star, moon, toe, and heel patterns (pgs. 118 and 119) to make appliqués. Fuse appliqués to stocking front.

5. Use 6 strands of floss to work Running Stitch along inner edges of toe and heel appliqués and 2 strands to work Running Stitch along edges of star and moon appliqués.

6. For hanger, fuse web to fabric. Cut a 3" x 6½" fabric strip. Finger press long edges 1" to wrong side; fuse in place. Fold in half to form a loop.

7. Place stocking pieces right sides together. Leaving top edge open, sew together along drawn lines. Clip seam allowance at curves, press top edge ½" to wrong side, and turn right side out. Repeat for lining, but do not turn lining. Place lining in stocking. Pin 1" of ends of hanger between stocking and lining at heel side of stocking. Pin top edges of stocking and lining together. Use 6 strands of floss to work a Running Stitch along top edge of stocking, catching hanger in stitching.

8. Glue buttons and greenery sprig to stocking.

DIAGRAM

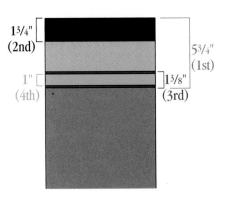

the more the MERRIER

*W*hen your list of people to remember is as long as Santa's, look to our captivating collection of small gifts. It's as easy to make several as it is one with this sleighload of inexpensive projects! There are cheery painted candle holders, scented wax ornaments, embroidered towels, festive pins, nostalgic notebooks, holiday memo cubes, and much more. With such a terrific variety of handmade presents, you can express your appreciation to everyone from co-workers and club members to school friends and extended family. Gift-giving will be a breeze this Noel as you spread joy all around!

43

...ENTS

Expect to Spe...

ornaments (6 pack)
paint pen
ribbon

Total for 6 gifts
Each gift

WHAT TO B...

Box of 6 red glass ornaments
Green paint pen
5 yd spool ½"w ribbon

THINGS YOU
HAVE AT HOME

Tracing paper, transfer paper,
stylus, cups, and a gold paint pen

TECHNIQUES
YOU'LL NEED

Patterns (pg. 98)

Finished in minutes, plain glass balls are transformed into striking ornaments using paint pens and ribbon hangers. The tree-trimmers make splendid gifts for party guests, co-workers, and other groups.

PAINTED GLASS ORNAMENTS

1. Transfer design (pg. 67) onto ornament.

2. (**Note:** Place ornament in cup to hold while painting and drying.) Use paint pens to paint over transferred lines and paint additional embellishments on ornament.

3. Thread a length of ribbon through ornament hanger and knot ends.

44

POTPOURRI PRETTIES

Expect to Spend

orange slices (10 pack)	3.47
cinnamon sticks (2.1 oz.)	1.67
cloves (.62 oz.)	3.96
bay leaves (.12 oz.)	2.18
essential oil (.33 oz.)	2.96
Shaker boxes	6.45
ribbon	10.99
paint	2.91
pinecone picks	2.50

Total for 5 gifts	$37.09
Each gift	$7.42

WHAT TO BUY

1 small bag (10 pack) dried
  orange slices
1 package (2.1 oz.) cinnamon
  sticks
1 container (.62 oz.) whole cloves
1 container (.12 oz.) bay leaves
1 bottle (.33 oz.) sweet orange
  essential oil
5 approx. 4³/8" dia. Shaker boxes
10 yd spool 2"w velvet wired
  ribbon
Ivory, burgundy, and metallic gold
  acrylic paint
5 gold pinecone picks
  (2 pinecones per pick)

THINGS YOU
HAVE AT HOME

Paintbrushes, paper towels, and
glue

TECHNIQUES
YOU'LL NEED

Painting (pg. 100)

*A*dd a fragrant touch to friends'
homes with gifts of holiday potpourri.
A bowlful of the spicy orange-scented
mixture will let you fill five little boxes
topped with elegant wired ribbon and
golden pinecones.

ORANGE POTPOURRI

1. Paint gold accents on orange slices and
cinnamon sticks. Break cinnamon sticks
into pieces to fit in box.

2. Place orange slices, cinnamon sticks,
cloves, and bay leaves in a bowl. Add
several drops of essential oil and gently
mix.

POTPOURRI BOXES

1. Paint inside of box and lid burgundy.
Paint outside of box and lid ivory. Dry
brush box and lid gold.

2. Measure box (**Fig. 1**, pg. 66). Cut a
length of ribbon this size. Center and glue
ribbon around box with ends to inside.
Repeat to glue ribbon to lid. Tie a length of
ribbon into a bow; trim ends. Glue bow and
1 pinecone to lid.

(Continued on pg. 66)

45

STARRY CANDLE HOLDERS

Expect to Spend

candle holders	3.96
raffia	1.99
cinnamon sticks (1½ oz.)	.99
candles	.80
Total for 4 gifts	**$7.74**
Each gift	**$1.94**

UNDER $5!

WHAT TO BUY

4 clear glass votive candle holders
Red raffia
Cinnamon sticks
4 white votive candles

THINGS YOU HAVE AT HOME

Tracing paper, compressed craft sponge, permanent felt-tip pen, red and green acrylic paint, paper plate, paper towels, and glue (if needed)

TECHNIQUES YOU'LL NEED

Patterns (pg. 98)
Painting (pg. 100)

*I*nspired by starry nights, our little Yuletide twinklers are sweet tokens of appreciation for daycare providers or Sunday school teachers. Clear glass candle holders are sponge-painted with star motifs and then tied with raffia bows and aromatic cinnamon sticks.

SPONGE-PAINTED CANDLE HOLDERS
1. Make star pattern (pg. 67). Use pattern to cut star from sponge. Cut a small square from sponge.

2. Use star sponge to paint red stars on candle holder. Use square sponge to sponge green paint on rim of holder.

3. Break a cinnamon stick to about the same length as height of holder. Knot three lengths of raffia around holder and tie ends into a bow around cinnamon stick. If necessary, use a dot of glue to secure.

4. Put candle in holder.

NOSTALGIC NOTEBOOKS

Expect to Spend

notebooks	5.00
ribbon	5.99
wrapping paper	1.99
watercolor paper	2.50
Total for 5 gifts	**$15.48**
Each gift	**$3.10**

WHAT TO BUY

5 approx. 4¹/₄" x 5¹/₂" notebooks
About 1²/₃ yds 1³/₈"w ribbon
Santa-motif wrapping paper
1 sheet watercolor paper

THINGS YOU HAVE AT HOME

Glue

UNDER $5!

These jolly journals are ideal for recording fond memories, jotting down Christmas card mailing lists, and so much more! Decked with festive ribbon bands and nostalgic St. Nick cutouts, the small notebooks are nifty gifts for teachers and co-workers.

PERSONAL NOTEBOOKS

1. With ends meeting at center front, glue a length of ribbon around front cover of notebook.

2. For Santa, cut motif from wrapping paper and glue to watercolor paper. Tear motif from paper. Glue motif over ribbon ends on notebook.

47

STAMPED STATIONERY

Expect to Spend

folder	.25
fabric	.99
card stock paper	.45
rubber stamps (3 pack)	2.97
note cards and envelopes (12 pack)	5.98
gift cards (12 pack)	1.99
Total for 2 gifts	**$12.63**
Each gift	**$6.32**

WHAT TO BUY

9¹/₂" x 11⁵/₈" plain school folder
with pockets
¹/₄ yd fabric
3 sheets of card stock paper (we
used light brown and blue)
Set of 3 mini rubber stamps with
holiday designs
Set of 12 approx. 4¹/₂" x 6" plain
note cards with envelopes
Set of 12 approx. 2¹/₂" x 3⁷/₈"
plain gift cards

THINGS YOU HAVE AT HOME

Fusible web, black felt-tip pen,
serrated-cut craft scissors, glue,
black ink pad, and jute twine or
string

TECHNIQUES YOU'LL NEED

Fusible Products (pg. 98)

*S*ending Christmas greetings and
thank-you notes will be a snap for those
receiving your hand-embellished
stationery. By mixing two sizes of note
cards and envelopes, you can assemble
two handy gift sets decorated with rubber
stamping and fused fabric.

"HOLIDAY NOTES" SETS

1. (Note: Refer to **Fig. 1** for Step 1.) For
stationery folders, cut 7¹/₂" from each side
of folder; discard center section. For
stationery pockets, trim areas shown in
dark blue from folder pockets. Cut slits in
stationery pockets for gift cards (shown in

red). Fold each folder section in half from
top to bottom (folders will have pockets on
opposite sides).

Fig. 1

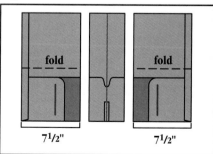

fold   fold

7¹/₂"   7¹/₂"

(Continued on pg. 66)

REFRESHING BATH SETS

WHAT TO BUY

4 lb. box Epsom salts
5 lb. box rock salt
1 bottle (.33 oz.) sweet orange
   essential oil
4 sisal bath mitts
Four 2¹/₄"w wooden star cutouts
Metallic gold spray paint
4 oz. eucalyptus
Stems of preserved cedar

THINGS YOU HAVE AT HOME

Food coloring (optional), 4 large
resealable plastic bags, glue, small
twigs, jute twine or string, and
raffia

*B*athtime will be a super soothing
experience with our refreshing bath
salts and mitts. With just one batch
of homemade bath salts, you can
present four gifts of store-bought mitts
embellished with fragrant naturals.

BATH SALTS

Combine 6 cups Epsom salts, 3 cups rock
salt, and several drops of essential oil in a
large bowl; mix thoroughly. If desired, add
several drops of food coloring and mix
well. Divide mixture into plastic bags.

DECORATED BATH MITTS

1. Spray paint stars gold.

2. For each decoration, glue several stems
of eucalyptus and cedar and several twigs
together into a bundle. Use a length of jute
to knot bundle to hanger of bath mitt. Tie
several lengths of jute and raffia into a bow.
Glue bow and star to bundle.

3. Place a bag of bath salts in mitt.

CLOTHESPIN ANGELS

To herald the holidays, crochet a host of these heavenly ornaments! Our easy little clothespin angels are quick and inexpensive to craft for everyone you hold dear.

WHAT TO BUY

White and Red bedspread weight cotton thread (each angel uses 15 yds of White and 28 yds of Red; we used 1 ball each of White and Red DMC Cebelia thread)
Nine ³/₄" dia. x 3³/₄" long round wooden craft clothespins
2 yds ¹/₈"w satin ribbon

THINGS YOU HAVE AT HOME

Crochet hook, size 5 (1.90 mm) or size needed for gauge; and glue

TECHNIQUES YOU'LL NEED

Crochet (pg. 104)

CROCHETED ANGELS

GAUGE: 16 dc and 8 rows = 2"

BODICE

With Red and leaving 18" at beginning for Neck Edging, ch 14 **loosely**; being careful not to twist ch, join with slip st to form a ring.

Rnd 1 (Right side): Ch 3 **(counts as first dc, now and throughout)**, dc in same st, 2 dc in next ch, † ch 1, (dc, ch 1) 3 times in next ch, (dc, ch 1) twice in next ch, (dc, ch 1) 3 times in next ch †, 2 dc in each of next 4 chs, repeat from † to † once, 2 dc in each of last 2 chs; join with slip st to first dc: 32 dc.

Note: Loop a short piece of thread around any stitch to mark last round as **right** side.

Rnd 2: Ch 3, dc in next 3 dc, ch 1, skip next 9 ch-1 sps (Armhole), dc in next 8 dc, ch 1, skip next 9 ch-1 sps (Armhole), dc in last 4 dc; join with slip st to first dc: 16 dc.

SKIRT

Rnd 1: Ch 6, working in each dc and in each ch around, dc in same st, ch 3, dc in next dc, ★ (ch 3, dc) twice in next st, ch 3, dc in next st; repeat from ★ around, ch 1, dc in third ch of beginning ch-6 to form last sp: 27 sps.

Rnds 2-10: Sc in same sp, (ch 3, sc in next ch-3 sp) around, ch 1, dc in first sc to form last sp.

Rnd 11: Sc in same sp, ch 3, (sc in next ch-3 sp, ch 3) around; join with slip st to first sc, finish off.

EDGING

To work **Cluster**, ch 3, YO, insert hook in third ch from hook, YO and pull up a loop, YO and draw through 2 loops on hook, YO, insert hook in same ch, YO and pull up a loop, YO and draw through 2 loops on hook, YO and draw through all 3 loops on hook.

With **right** side facing, join White with sc in first ch-3 sp (see Joining with sc); work Cluster, (sc in next ch-3 sp, work Cluster) around; join with slip st to first sc, finish off.

WING

Rnd 1: With **right** side facing and working in free loop of ch-1 and in skipped ch-1 sps of Armhole, join White with sc in ch-1 at underarm; ch 3, sc around post of next dc, ch 3, (sc in next ch-1 sp, ch 3) 9 times, sc around post of next dc, ch 1, dc in first sc to form last sp: 12 sps.

Rnds 2 and 3: Sc in same sp, (ch 3, sc in next ch-3 sp) around, ch 1, dc in first sc to form last sp.

Rnd 4: Sc in same sp, work Cluster, (sc in next ch-3 sp, work Cluster) around; join with slip st to first sc, finish off.

Repeat for second Wing.

HALO

Rnd 1 (Right side): With Red, ch 2, 8 sc in second ch from hook; join with slip st to first sc.

Rnd 2: Ch 1, sc in same st, (ch 3, sc in next sc) around, ch 1, dc in first sc to form last sp: 8 sps.

Rnd 3: Sc in same sp, ch 4, (sc in next ch-3 sp, ch 4) around; join with slip st to first sc, finish off.

FINISHING

NECK EDGING

With **right** side facing and working in free loops of beginning ch, insert hook in same ch as joining, using beginning length, YO and pull up a loop; (ch 1, slip st in next ch) around; finish off.

Weave ribbon through sts on Rnd 2 of Bodice. Put dress on clothespin and tie ribbon into a bow. Glue Halo to angel head.

SCENTED WAX ORNAMENTS

WHAT TO BUY

2 lb. pre-colored wax block (we
  used green)
1 package (.5 oz.) of candle scent
  squares
Cookie or craft mold (our
  ceramic cookie mold
  measures about 4⁷/₈"h)
Wax release spray
10 yd spool ¹/₄"w ribbon for
  hangers
3¹/₃ yds ⁵/₈"w ribbon for bows

THINGS YOU
HAVE AT HOME

Newspapers, large can and a pan
or electric skillet to melt wax,
uncoated floral wire or paper
clips, wire cutters, and waxed
paper

*Whether used as a tree ornament
or a room freshener, our scented wax
evergreen will add a touch of Christmas
charm to the holiday season. A single
block of wax will make about ten gifts,
depending on the size of your ceramic
cookie or craft mold.*

SCENTED WAX ORNAMENTS

1. Apply wax release to mold.

2. (**Caution:** When melting wax, do not
place can directly on burner.) Cover work
area with newspaper. Place can in pan on
stove or in electric skillet; fill pan or skillet
half full with water. Melt wax in can. Add
scent to wax.

3. Carefully pour wax into mold and allow
to harden slightly. For hanger, either form
an approx. 3" length of wire into a "U"
shape or unbend a paper clip once and cut
in half. With loop of hanger extending just
past top of wax shape, place hanger in wax.
If needed, add a small amount of additional
wax to completely cover bottom of hanger.
Allow wax to harden, then remove from
mold and place on waxed paper to cool
completely.

4. Loop a length of ¹/₄"w ribbon through
wire hanger; knot and trim ends. Tie a
⁵/₈"w ribbon length into a bow around
hanger.

CRAFTY BRAG BOOKS

UNDER $5!

WHAT TO BUY

3 photo albums to hold 3½" x 5"
  photos
⅓ yd fabric
2½"w wooden heart cutout
⅔ yd 1"w grosgrain ribbon
⅔ yd ⅛"w satin ribbon
1 yd ³⁄₁₆" dia. piping

THINGS YOU HAVE AT HOME

Batting, glue, fabric scraps,
buttons, and pinking shears

*O ur purse-size brag books are
terrific for carrying photos along on
holiday visits. We dressed plain photo
albums in three different styles
— each for less than $4 — so that
you can tailor them to the tastes of
various friends or relatives. Because
there's no sewing involved, this is
a great project for beginning crafters.*

PHOTO BRAG BOOKS

1. If possible, remove photo pages from
album. Measure length (from top to
bottom) and width of open album. Cut a
piece of batting this size. Cut a piece of
fabric 1" larger on all sides than batting.

2. With album closed, glue batting to
outside of album. Center open album on
wrong side of fabric piece. Glue corners of
fabric over corners of album. Glue edges of
fabric over edges of album, trimming to fit
around album hardware.

3. For ribbon trim, cut an 8" length of 1"w
ribbon; glue ribbon around album front,
wrapping ends to inside. For piping, glue
flange of piping along edges on inside of
album, overlapping ends at center bottom.
For ribbon ties, cut two 8" lengths of ⅛"w
ribbon; glue 1 end of 1 ribbon length to
inside front and 1 end of remaining length
to inside back cover of album.

(Continued on pg. 66)

53

SNOW PAL CANDLE HOLDERS

WHAT TO BUY

4 frosted-glass round votive
    candle holders
Orange and black dimensional
    paint
2/3 yd 7/8"w plaid ribbon
4 white votive candles

THINGS YOU HAVE AT HOME

Glue

TECHNIQUES YOU'LL NEED

Painting (pg. 100)

UNDER $5!

This frosty fellow's smile is sure to light up the room! The cute candle holder costs just over two dollars to craft, so you can make plenty to use as table decorations that double as party favors. A knotted ribbon "scarf" glued to the bottom of the glass cup lends a winsome touch to the wintry accent.

SNOWMAN CANDLE HOLDERS

1. For snowman, paint black squares on candle holder for eyes and black dots for mouth. Paint an orange triangle for nose.

2. For scarf, knot center of a 6" length of ribbon. For fringe, make clips in each end of ribbon. Glue knot of scarf to candle holder.

3. Put candle in holder.

MERRY MINI STOCKINGS

WHAT TO BUY

1/3 yd 54"w ecru felt
Yellow, pink, green, red, blue, and
    purple felt pieces
1 skein each yellow, green, and
    red embroidery floss
Box of 12 candy canes

THINGS YOU
HAVE AT HOME

Tracing paper, embroidery needle,
small buttons, and glue

TECHNIQUES
YOU'LL NEED

Patterns (pg. 98)
Embroidery (pg. 103)

When you need lots of merry little gifts, choose these quick-and-easy felt mini stockings — you can make two for less than a dollar! The sweet shapes are sewn together in a flash with decorative blanket stitching, and the cuffs and felt posies are simply glued on.

FELT STOCKINGS

1. Make patterns (pg. 120). Use patterns to cut shapes from felt.

2. Place stocking pieces together. Use 3 strands of floss to work Blanket Stitch along edges of stocking, leaving top edge open.

3. Use floss to sew button to center of daisy. Glue posy center to posy; use 3 strands of floss to work Blanket Stitch along edges of posy center. Glue 1 leaf to back of each flower. Glue cuff and flowers to stocking.

4. For hanger, fold a 1/2" x 4" felt strip in half and glue ends inside top of stocking.

CHRISTMAS CARD BOOKMARKS

Expect to Spend

card stock paper	.75
vinyl	1.27
Total for up to 20 gifts	**$2.02**
Each gift	**$.10**

WHAT TO BUY

Five 8¹/2" x 11" sheets of card stock paper (we used 5 different colors)
1 yd matte-finish clear iron-on vinyl

THINGS YOU HAVE AT HOME

Colored paper scraps (optional), glue, Christmas cards, colored pencils, black felt-tip pen, gold paint pen, and a pressing cloth

TECHNIQUES YOU'LL NEED

Fusible Products (pg. 98)

When you can't bear to throw away those beautiful Christmas cards received over the years, recycle them into bookmarks! Quick, easy, and inexpensive (only ten cents apiece), the vinyl-covered page keepers make wonderful tokens for large groups at school or church.

RECYCLED CARD BOOKMARKS

1. Cut a strip from card stock paper for bookmark. If a second color of background is desired, cut a strip from colored paper slightly smaller than bookmark and glue to bookmark. Either cutting along edges of design, cutting small pieces from design, or cutting a strip from design, cut piece(s) from card to fit on bookmark and glue to bookmark.

2. Use colored pencils, black pen, and paint pen to decorate bookmark and write message if desired.

3. Cut 2 vinyl strips about ¹/4" larger on all sides than bookmark. Center bookmark between strips and use pressing cloth to fuse strips together. Trim vinyl close to bookmark.

"LET IT SNOW" DOOR PILLOWS

Expect to Spend

fabric	2.73
ribbon	.50
pom-poms (40 pack)	.49

Total for 7 gifts	**$3.72**
Each gift	**$.53**

WHAT TO BUY

Fabric:
- 1/4 yd muslin
- 1/4 yd blue
- 1/4 yd red
- 1/8 yd white
- 10 yd spool 1/4"w green ribbon
- 5mm white pom-poms

THINGS YOU HAVE AT HOME

White acrylic paint, toothbrush, paintbrush, fusible web, pressing cloth, fabric scraps for remaining appliqués, black felt-tip pen, thread to match fabrics, and polyester fiberfill

TECHNIQUES YOU'LL NEED

Fusible Products (pg. 98)
Appliqué (pg. 99)
Painting (pg. 100)

*T*rimming the entryway will never be sweeter than with these "a-door-able" mini pillows. With some scraps and just a quarter yard each of several fabrics, you can create seven of these charming door decorations for about fifty cents apiece.

DOOR PILLOWS

1. Cut a 51/2" x 71/2" piece from blue fabric for pillow front and a 51/2" x 71/2" piece from muslin for pillow back.

2. For snow on pillow front, use toothbrush and white paint to spatter paint blue fabric piece.

3. Fuse web to wrong sides of red fabric and remaining muslin. Cut two 11/4" x 71/2" and two 11/4" x 51/2" strips from red fabric and four 11/4" squares from muslin for trim on pillow front. Using pressing cloth, fuse red strips along edges of pillow front and muslin squares to corners.

(Continued on pg. 66)

"NO POUTING ZONE" SIGNS

UNDER $5!

WHAT TO BUY

6 wooden door hangers
6 photocopies of sign design
   (pg. 120)
White dimensional paint

THINGS YOU HAVE AT HOME

Acrylic paint, paintbrushes, colored pencils, black felt-tip pen (optional), glue, and clear acrylic spray sealer

TECHNIQUES YOU'LL NEED

Painting (pg. 100)

There'll be no "bah humbugs" heard around the neighborhood when every home displays this cheery little door sign. Using wooden door hangers and photocopies of the pattern we've provided, you can make six happy hangers for under two dollars apiece.

DOOR SIGNS

1. Paint basecoat on hanger.

2. Use colored pencils to color photocopy of sign. If desired, use pen to draw over black lines. Cut out sign and glue to hanger.

3. Use dimensional paint to paint snow at top and bottom of sign and snowflakes in background.

4. Spray sign with sealer.

58

CHARMING BIBS

WHAT TO BUY

2 bibs to hold an approx. 6" x 7"
and a 5" x 6" design (we used
red and green trimmed
Janlynn® bibs)
¹/₄ yd green fabric
¹/₈ yd each of red and brown
fabric

THINGS YOU
HAVE AT HOME

Fusible web, fusible tear-away
stabilizer, clear nylon thread
and thread to match bib, black
permanent felt-tip pen, white
and black embroidery floss,
embroidery needle, and glue
(if needed)

TECHNIQUES
YOU'LL NEED

Patterns (pg. 98)
Fusible Products (pg. 98)
Appliqué (pg. 99)
Embroidery (pg. 103)

UNDER $5!

*Make mealtime fun for young
ones with our festive appliquéd bibs.
Decorated with a wreath or reindeer
motif, the bibs will keep little mess-
makers neat and clean for receiving
all those holiday hugs.*

REINDEER BIB

1. Use deer, collar, and grass patterns
(pg. 121) to make appliqués. Arrange
appliqués on bib and fuse in place.

2. Use clear thread to stitch appliqués in
place.

3. Use pen to draw antlers and mouth on
deer.

4. Use 6 strands each of white and black
floss together to work a French Knot for
eye.

WREATH BIB

1. Use wreath and bow patterns (pg. 118)
to make appliqués. Make a vertical cut
through top of wreath appliqué; press cut
edges about ³/₄" to wrong side. Place
wreath appliqué at center top of bib and
fold pressed edges to back. Fuse wreath in
place, including edges folded to back. Fuse
bow appliqué to bib at bottom of wreath. If
necessary, glue pressed edges of wreath in
place on back of bib.

2. Use clear thread to stitch appliqués in
place.

3. Use pen to draw detail lines on bow.

COUNTRY CHRISTMAS PINS

WHAT TO BUY

3 white felt pieces
Fabric:
 1/8 yd peach
 1/4 yd muslin
6 cards of 7 black buttons each
1" long pin backs
Santa Pins:
1/8 yd red checked fabric
Angel Pins:
1/8 yd red checked fabric
Package of 22-gauge uncoated
 floral wire lengths

THINGS YOU HAVE AT HOME

Fusible web, black felt-tip pen,
red crayon, and glue
Santa Pins: black thread
Angel Pins: 1/2" x 7" torn fabric
strips for bows, a large nail, wire
cutters, and ecru thread

TECHNIQUES YOU'LL NEED

Fusible Products (pg. 98)
Appliqué (pg. 99)

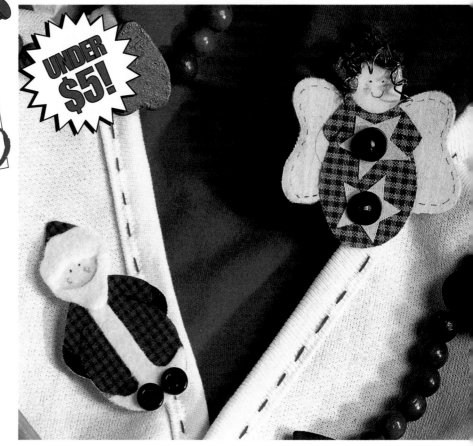

For less than fifty cents each, you can share these Yuletide pins with everyone! The tiny treasures are brimming with country appeal.

SANTA PINS

1. Fuse muslin to 1 side of 1 felt piece. Use patterns (pg. 121) to make appliqués, making beard, hat trim, and coat trim from another felt piece. Arrange and fuse appliqués to side of first felt piece opposite muslin. Cut out Santa.

2. Use black pen to draw dots for eyes and lines on suit for arms. Use crayon to color cheeks.

3. Sew 2 buttons to Santa for boots.

4. Glue pin back to back of Santa.

ANGEL PINS

1. Fuse muslin to 1 side of 1 felt piece. Use patterns (pg. 121) to make appliqués. Arrange and fuse appliqués to side of felt piece opposite muslin. Cut out angel.

2. Use black pen to draw eyes, mouth, stitches on wings, and lines on dress for arms. Use crayon to color cheeks.

3. Tie torn fabric strip into a bow; trim ends. Glue bow to head.

4. For hair, cut 1 wire length in half. Wrap 1 short wire length around nail to curl; remove wire from nail. Curve curly wire length to fit along top of head and cut to fit. Glue to angel.

5. Sew buttons to stars on angel.

6. Glue pin back to back of angel.

SENSATIONAL TOWELS

Expect to Spend

towels	5.94
ribbon	4.47
Total for 2 gifts	**$10.41**
Each gift	**$5.21**

WHAT TO BUY

2 white fingertip towels (we used Charles Craft® Cross Stitch Collection towels)

3 yd package each dark yellow (53), red (49), and green (19) YLI 7mm silk ribbon

THINGS YOU HAVE AT HOME

White tissue paper, embroidery needle, thread, and tweezers (if needed)

TECHNIQUES YOU'LL NEED

Silk Ribbon Embroidery (pg. 103)

A little bit of silk ribbon embroidery is all it takes to brighten fingertip towels for holiday hostess gifts. Providing the appeal of delicate handwork, the Yuletide designs are really quite easy to complete.

RIBBON EMBROIDERED TOWELS

1. Trace embroidery pattern (pg. 67) onto tissue paper; cut out pattern about 1" outside design. Position pattern on towel and baste in place.

2. Referring to Stitch Guide (pg. 67), stitch design over pattern on towel. Using tweezers if necessary, remove pattern from towel.

STAMPED MEMO CUBES

WHAT TO BUY

5 memo cubes
3 mini rubber stamps

THINGS YOU HAVE AT HOME

Black ink pad, felt-tip pens, and curling ribbon

UNDER $5!

Jotting down notes will be extra nice for co-workers who receive these jolly memo cubes. For the desk-friendly gifts, simply stamp the sides of plain paper cubes with holiday motifs and color them using felt-tip pens.

STAMPED MEMO CUBES

1. Use stamps and ink pad to stamp designs on sides of cube. Use pens to color designs.

2. Tie curling ribbon around cube and curl ends.

FLOWERPOT WRAPS

WHAT TO BUY

4 small plants in approx. 3¼"h
  pots
1 yd fabric
9 yds of gold mini star garland
Package of heavy-gauge floral wire
  lengths
4 plastic Christmas ornaments

THINGS YOU
HAVE AT HOME

4 small plastic bags, 4 rubber
bands, glue, wire cutters, and
needle-nose pliers

*G*reat gifts for friends with green
thumbs, small potted plants are simple
to dress up with holiday fabric and
starry garland. Ornaments dangling
from lengths of heavy wire make festive
plant pokes.

POUFY SEASONAL POT COVERS
1. Measure pot from 1 side of rim to
opposite side of rim (**Fig. 1**); multiply
by 2. Cut a fabric square this size.

Fig. 1

(Continued on pg. 66)

63

EMBELLISHED PAPER FRAMES

Expect to Spend

frames	5.07
fabric	1.00
rickrack	1.19
wire (20 pack)	.99
Total for 3 gifts	**$8.25**
Each gift	**$2.75**

WHAT TO BUY

3 brown paper-covered frames to
hold 3¹/₂" x 5" photos
¹/₈ yd white fabric for snowman
and wings on angel
Snowman Frame:
¹/₈ yd fabric for border
Angel Frame:
Package of white baby rickrack
Package of 22-gauge uncoated
floral wire lengths

THINGS YOU HAVE AT HOME

Fabric scraps for additional
appliqués, fusible web, poster
board, black felt-tip pen, and glue
Snowman Frame: 3 small
buttons
Angel Frame: 2 small buttons, a
large nail, and wire cutters
Holly Frame: ribbon for bow

TECHNIQUES YOU'LL NEED

Fusible Products (pg. 98)
Appliqué (pg. 99)

*I*nexpensive paper-covered frames are
quick and easy to personalize with
colorful trims and handwriting. With our
three designs, you can create unique
frames for lots of people on your gift list.

SNOWMAN FRAME
1. Use snowman, hat, nose, scarf, heart,
pom-pom, and scarf end patterns (pg. 120)
to make appliqués. Arrange and fuse
appliqués to poster board. Cut out
snowman.

2. Use pen to draw eyes and mouth on
snowman.

3. Fuse web to wrong side of fabric for
border. Cut ¹/₂"w strips to fit along edges of
frame opening. Overlapping ends, fuse
strips around frame opening. Glue
snowman to frame. Glue buttons to
remaining corners of border.

4. Use pen to personalize frame.

(Continued on pg. 66)

SMILING FACES

WHAT TO BUY

12" x 18" piece black Aida
   (14 ct)
Embroidery floss (see color key,
   pg. 67)
Three 2¹/₂" dia. red Flexi-hoop™
   embroidery frames
³/₄ yd ¹/₄"w ribbon

THINGS YOU HAVE AT HOME

Tapestry needle, chalk pencil, felt
scraps for backing, and glue

TECHNIQUES YOU'LL NEED

Cross Stitch (pg. 102)

All smiles, our playful cross-stitched characters make jolly little gifts — and you can stitch all three for under $7! Because the Yuletide whimsies are quick and easy, you'll have time to make plenty for Christmas giving.

HOLIDAY FACES ORNAMENTS
1. Referring to chart and color key (pg. 67), stitch design on a 5" square of Aida. Use 3 strands of floss for Cross Stitch and 1 for Backstitch.

2. For backing, use chalk pencil to draw around inner ring of frame on felt. Cut out circle. Center stitched piece in frame and replace inner ring. Trim edges of stitched piece close to inner ring. Glue backing over back of stitched piece.

3. Tie a ribbon length into a bow around hanger on frame; trim ends.

POTPOURRI PRETTIES
(Continued from pg. 45)

Fig. 1

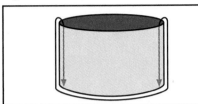

3. Place some potpourri and a pinecone in box. Aligning ribbon lengths, place lid on box.

STAMPED STATIONERY
(Continued from pg. 48)

2. To cover inside of each folder, fuse web to wrong side of fabric. Cut a piece of fabric to fit inside folder. Fuse fabric into folder behind pocket.

3. For each label, use black pen to write "Holiday Notes" on card stock paper. Use craft scissors to cut out label. Glue label to another color of card stock paper and cut out. Glue label to fabric and cut out. Fuse to front of folder.

4. For paper cutouts, stamp designs on card stock paper, leaving about 3/4" between designs. Cut out designs in desired shapes. Glue to note cards, envelopes, gifts cards, and folders.

5. For fabric cutouts, cut desired shapes from fabric and fuse to cards and folders.

6. Use black pen to draw dots and stitches on cards, envelopes, gift cards, and folders.

7. Place 6 cards, 6 envelopes, and 6 gift cards in each folder. Tie a length of twine into a bow around each folder.

CRAFTY BRAG BOOKS
(Continued from pg. 53)

4. Cut 2 pieces of fabric same size as front of album. Press edges about 1/4" to wrong side. Center and glue 1 fabric piece inside front and 1 inside back of album.

5. For bow, tie remaining 1"w ribbon into a bow; glue bow to front of album. For padded heart, draw around wooden heart on batting and wrong side of fabric. Cut out batting heart just inside drawn lines. Cut out fabric heart 1/2" outside drawn lines. Center batting heart, then wooden heart, on wrong side of fabric heart. Glue edges of fabric to wrong side of heart. Beginning at top, glue flange of piping along edges on back of heart. Glue heart to album. Tie a length of 1/8"w ribbon into a bow and glue to heart. For fabric patches and buttons, use pinking shears to cut small squares from fabrics; glue squares and buttons to album front.

6. If pages were removed, return them to album.

"LET IT SNOW" DOOR PILLOWS
(Continued from pg. 57)

4. Use snowman, hat, nose, scarf, heart, and star patterns (pg. 120) to make appliqués. Using pressing cloth, fuse appliqués to pillow front.

5. Use white paint and paintbrush to paint snowman arms and "Let it SNOW" on pillow front. Use pen to draw eyes and mouth on snowman.

6. Tear a 1/2" x 5" fabric strip for scarf. Knot strip at center; glue knot to one side of scarf appliqué. Glue pom-pom to hat.

7. Matching right sides, use a 1/4" seam allowance to sew pillow front and back together, leaving an opening for turning. Clip corners, turn right side out, and press. Lightly stuff with fiberfill. Hand sew opening closed.

8. Press ends of a 13 1/2" ribbon length 1/2" to 1 side. Tack pressed ends to top corners on back of pillow.

FLOWERPOT WRAPS
(Continued from pg. 63)

2. Place pot of plant in plastic bag. Center pot on wrong side of fabric square. Bring edges of fabric up and fold to inside of bag. Place rubber band around fabric, bag, and pot just below rim of pot. Glue fabric in place around rim.

3. Wrap a length of garland several times around pot to cover rubber band.

4. Cut an approx. 8" length from 1 wire length; use pliers to bend 1 end into a hook shape. Place ornament on hook and twist wire to secure. Insert wire into pot.

EMBELLISHED PAPER FRAMES
(Continued from pg. 64)

ANGEL FRAME

1. Use angel body, wing, dress, and star patterns (pg. 121) to make appliqués. Arrange and fuse appliqués to poster board. Cut out angel.

2. Use pen to draw face, lines on dress for arms, and stitches on wings.

3. For hair, cut a wire length in half. Wrap 1 short wire length around nail to curl. Remove wire from nail. Curve curly wire length to fit along top of head and cut to fit. Glue to angel. Glue buttons to angel.

4. Glue rickrack along inner edges of frame. Glue angel to frame.

5. Use pen to personalize frame.

HOLLY FRAME

1. Use leaf, berry, and star patterns (pg. 120) to make appliqués. Fuse star to poster board; cut out. Arrange and fuse remaining appliqués to frame.

2. Tie ribbon into a bow; trim ends. Glue bow to frame. Glue star to bow.

3. Use pen to personalize frame.

SPLENDID ORNAMENTS
(pg. 44)

SMILING FACES
(pg. 65)

STARRY CANDLE HOLDERS
(pg. 46)

SENSATIONAL TOWELS
(pg. 61)

STITCH GUIDE		
STITCH NAME	SYMBOL	YLI
Chain Stitch		19
Lazy Daisy Stitch		49
Japanese Ribbon Stitch		19
		49
Straight Stitch	—	49
French Knot		49
		53

X	DMC	¼X	B'ST	ANC.	COLOR
	blanc			2	white
	ecru			387	ecru
	310			403	black
	498			1005	dk red
	666			46	red
	721			324	orange
	754			1012	flesh
	775			128	lt blue
	798			131	blue
	909			923	dk green
	911			205	green
	913			204	lt green
	3716			25	pink

festive FLAIR

*W*ith the sensational styles found in our clothing collection, you can add festive flair to anyone's wardrobe! You'll have a blast creating thrifty holiday fashions such as whimsical vests and sweet shirts for family and friends. There are wearables for wee ones, too, including fanciful footwear, a sponge-painted romper, and a cheery appliquéd cardigan. Helping others accessorize for the season will be a snap with our cross-stitched socks, embroidered pins, and cozy crocheted hat and mitten set. These good-looking gifts will never go out of style!

LI'L DEER CARDIGAN

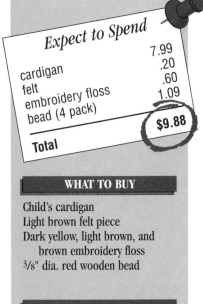
WHAT TO BUY

Child's cardigan
Light brown felt piece
Dark yellow, light brown, and
  brown embroidery floss
3/8" dia. red wooden bead

THINGS YOU HAVE AT HOME

Yellow felt scrap for moon
appliqué, fusible web, black
embroidery floss, and an
embroidery needle

TECHNIQUES YOU'LL NEED

Appliqué (pg. 99)
Embroidery (pg. 103)

This cardigan is a cute cover-up for a dear little one. Wandering beneath a cheery crescent moon, our friendly reindeer will lead the way to Christmas glee! The felt appliqués are edged with simple blanket stitching.

REINDEER CARDIGAN

1. Wash, dry, and press cardigan and felt.

2. Use deer and moon patterns (pg. 121) to make appliqués. Arrange appliqués on cardigan and fuse in place.

3. Use 3 strands of dark yellow floss to work Blanket Stitch along edges of moon. Use 3 strands of brown floss to work Blanket Stitch along edges of reindeer. Use 3 strands of black floss to work French Knots for eyes and Straight Stitch for mouth. Use 6 strands of light brown floss to work Straight Stitches for antlers and to sew bead to reindeer for nose.

STAR-BRIGHT ROMPER

WHAT TO BUY

Child's romper

THINGS YOU HAVE AT HOME

Tracing paper; compressed craft sponge; black permanent felt-tip pen; yellow, red, and green acrylic paint; paper plates; paper towels; and a small T-shirt form

TECHNIQUES YOU'LL NEED

Patterns (pg. 98)
Painting (pg. 100)

The star of this holiday season will be our jaunty sponge-painted romper! Finished in four easy steps, the playsuit is enhanced with pen "stitching."

HOLIDAY ROMPER

1. Wash, dry, and press romper.

2. Make patterns (pg. 121). Use patterns to cut shapes from sponge.

3. Use sponge shapes to paint red candy canes, yellow stars, and green rectangles on jumper.

4. Use pen to draw stitches around stars and stripes on candy canes.

COZY HAT & MITTENS

UNDER $5!

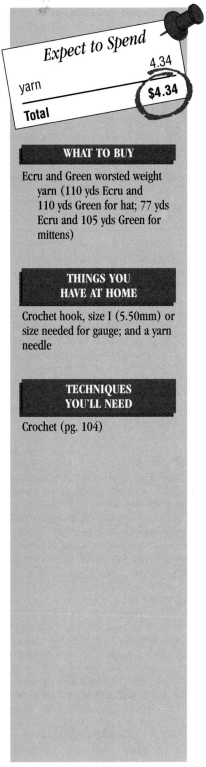

Expect to Spend

yarn	4.34
Total	**$4.34**

WHAT TO BUY

Ecru and Green worsted weight
  yarn (110 yds Ecru and
  110 yds Green for hat; 77 yds
  Ecru and 105 yds Green for
  mittens)

THINGS YOU
HAVE AT HOME

Crochet hook, size I (5.50mm) or
size needed for gauge; and a yarn
needle

TECHNIQUES
YOU'LL NEED

Crochet (pg. 104)

*D*onning our cozy crocheted hat and
mittens, your favorite winter weather
enthusiast will stay warm and toasty.
What a nice way to show you care!

CROCHETED HAT AND MITTENS
Gauge: 7 sc and 8 rows (4 stripes) = 2"

HAT
Note: Work in BLO throughout all rows.
With Ecru, ch 40 **loosely.**
Row 1 (Wrong side): Sc in second ch
from hook and in each ch across changing
to Green in last sc; do **not** cut Ecru: 39 sc.

Row 2: Ch 1, turn; sc in first 34 sc, leave
remaining 5 sc unworked: 34 sc.

Row 3: Turn; skip first sc, sc in each sc
across changing to Ecru in last sc; do **not**
cut Green: 33 sc.

Row 4: Ch 1, turn; sc first 33 sc, sc in end
of first row of last Green stripe and in
remaining 5 sc of previous Ecru stripe:
39 sc.

Row 5: Ch 1, turn; sc in same st and in
each sc across changing to Green in last sc

Row 6: Ch 1, turn; sc in first 29 sc, leave
remaining 10 sc unworked: 29 sc.

Row 7: Turn; skip first sc, sc in each sc
across changing to Ecru in last sc: 28 sc.

(Continued on pg. 82

TEACHER'S CHRISTMAS VEST

WHAT TO BUY

Adult's black felt vest
Dark yellow, green, and brown felt pieces
1/8 yd 70"w red felt
2 skeins red and 1 skein each white, dark yellow, green, and brown embroidery floss

THINGS YOU HAVE AT HOME

Tracing paper, glue, embroidery needle, tissue paper, buttons, pinking shears, chalk pencil, black thread, and tweezers (if needed)

TECHNIQUES YOU'LL NEED

Patterns (pg. 98)
Embroidery (pg. 103)

V is for this very merry vest that a teacher will enjoy! Enhanced with felt cutouts, hand stitching, and buttons, a ready-made felt vest makes an A⁺ gift for your child's favorite instructor.

TEACHER'S VEST

1. Wash, dry, and press vest and felt.

2. Make patterns (pg. 82). Use patterns to cut appliqués from felt. Cut two 5/8" x 4³/4" and two 5/8" x 5³/4" strips from brown felt for chalkboard frame appliqués. Arrange appliqués on vest; use dots of glue to secure.

3. (Note: Use 3 strands of floss and Running Stitch for Step 3.) Use matching floss to stitch along edges of apples (catching stems in stitching) and frame and along centers of leaves and highlights in apples. For words pattern, cut a 3¹/2" x 4¹/2" piece of tissue paper. With short edges at top and bottom, write the following at center of paper piece: Write Merry Christmas 100 times. Pin pattern in frame on vest. Use white floss to stitch words over pattern. Using tweezers if necessary, remove pattern from stitching. Use white floss to stitch star trails.

4. Use floss to sew buttons to stars and frame.

(Continued on pg. 82)

"COOL" SNOWMEN VEST

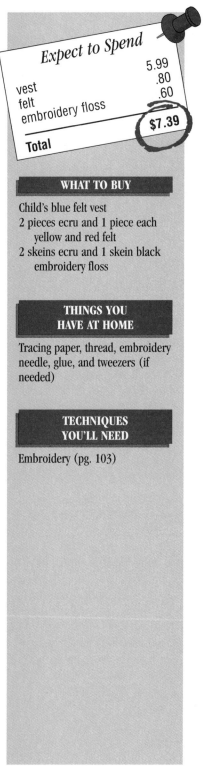

WHAT TO BUY

Child's blue felt vest
2 pieces ecru and 1 piece each
   yellow and red felt
2 skeins ecru and 1 skein black
   embroidery floss

THINGS YOU HAVE AT HOME

Tracing paper, thread, embroidery needle, glue, and tweezers (if needed)

TECHNIQUES YOU'LL NEED

Embroidery (pg. 103)

*F*or a little girl who loves fun clothing, this fashion accessory is truly "cool"! A ready-made felt vest is transformed into a playful piece for her winter wardrobe by adding appliquéd snow pals and decorative stitching.

SNOWMEN VEST

1. Wash, dry, and press vest and felt pieces.

2. Trace word patterns (pg. 122) onto tracing paper. Baste "Snowmen" pattern along bottom of right vest front. Stitching over pattern, use 4 strands of ecru floss to work Running Stitch over letters. Repeat to stitch "Are Cool" along bottom of left vest front. Using tweezers if necessary, remove pattern from stitching.

3. Make snowman patterns (pg. 122). Use patterns to cut appliqués from felt. Cut slit in large hat (shown in grey on pattern). Cut one 3/8" x 8" and one 3/8" x 9" strip from ecru felt for arms. Knot ends of strips.

4. Arrange appliqués on vest, placing head of large snowman into slit in hat and placing longer arms under large snowman. Use dots of glue to secure.

5. Use 2 strands of black floss to work Blanket Stitch along edges of snowmen, hats, scarf, and boots; French Knots for eyes; and Running Stitch for mouths and details on large snowman's hat. Whipstitch short edges of noses to faces. Use 4 strands of ecru floss to work Running Stitch along neck, front, and bottom edges of vest; work straight stitches for snowflakes on vest.

SNOWY SMILE T-SHIRT

WHAT TO BUY

Women's long-sleeve T-shirt
¼ yd black fabric
¼ yd red fabric

THINGS YOU HAVE AT HOME

Fabric scraps for nose and star appliqués, fusible web, fusible tear-away stabilizer, thread to match fabrics, safety pin, and a large button

TECHNIQUES YOU'LL NEED

Fusible Products (pg. 98)
Appliqué (pg. 99)

Wearing a winning smile and a stylish cloche, this darling snow woman is a breeze to create! All you do is machine appliqué her features onto a white T-shirt, and the frosty sweetheart is ready to share!

SNOW WOMAN SHIRT

1. Wash, dry, and press shirt and fabrics.

2. Use patterns (pg. 123) to make appliqués.

3. Arrange appliqués on shirt, spacing coal appliqués evenly with top one about 4½" below mouth; fuse in place.

4. Use matching thread to stitch appliqués in place and to stitch lines connecting corners of mouth to cheeks.

5. For ties on hat, cut two 3½" x 18" strips from red fabric. Press long edges, then ends of each strip ¼" to wrong side; press ¼" to wrong side again and stitch in place. Press an approx. ¼"w pleat in 1 end of each tie. Sew pleated ends of ties to shirt at sides of hat. Tie remaining ends into a bow. Use safety pin on inside of shirt to secure bow.

6. Sew button to star appliqué.

NIFTY NOEL FOOTWEAR

WHAT TO BUY

Fabric-Covered Shoes:
Children's slip-on canvas shoes
1/8 yd novelty Christmas fabric
1/3 yd 3/8"w grosgrain ribbon
White and red baby rickrack

Painted Shoes:
Children's slip-on shoes with straps
Small silk greenery pick
10 yd spool each yellow, red, and
   green 1/8"w satin ribbon
6 jingle bells

THINGS YOU HAVE AT HOME

Fabric-Covered Shoes:
newspaper, tracing paper, fusible
web, and glue **Painted Shoes:**
acrylic paint, paintbrushes, glue,
and wire cutters

TECHNIQUES YOU'LL NEED

Fusible Products (pg. 98)
Painting (pg. 100)

Little girls will love slipping into these sensational seasonal shoes! Plain footwear is easily enlivened with holly-jolly fabric, painted-on stripes, and other merry trims.

FABRIC-COVERED SHOES

1. Stuff toe of each shoe with newspaper until edge gathered with elastic is stretched flat. For each pattern, place tracing paper over toe of shoe and use a pencil to trace edges of part of shoe to be covered with fabric; cut out.

2. Fuse web to wrong side of fabric. Placing patterns over desired motifs on fabric, use patterns to cut appliqués for shoes. Fuse appliqués to shoes.

3. Glue ribbon over top raw edge of fabric on each shoe.

4. Twist white and red rickrack together. Glue lengths of rickrack along ribbon lengths and along bottom edges of shoes.

(Continued on pg. 83)

HANDSOME MUFFLER

UNDER $5!

WHAT TO BUY

¹/₃ yd of 60"w deep-pile polyester fleece

Skein of worsted weight yarn to match fleece

THINGS YOU HAVE AT HOME

Large tapestry needle

TECHNIQUES YOU'LL NEED

Embroidery (pg. 103)

*T*o make a nifty neck warmer in no time, start with a piece of soft, fuzzy fleece. Snipped at the ends to create fringe and edged with blanket stitching, this handsome scarf is sure to please a special gentleman friend.

FLEECE SCARF

1. If necessary, cut selvages from fleece. Cut a strip for scarf the desired width by the length of the fleece (we used the pattern in our fleece to determine the width of our 11¹/₂"w scarf).

2. For fringe, cut about 1" long clips at regular intervals in each end of scarf.

3. Use yarn to work Blanket Stitch along sides of scarf.

HOLLY-JOLLY APRON

WHAT TO BUY

Red apron
3 silk holly picks [with about 11
   large (about 3¹/₄" long) and 5
   medium (about 2¹/₄" long)
   leaves]
²/₃ yd 1¹/₂"w ribbon
Gold glitter dimensional paint
5 large red buttons

THINGS YOU HAVE AT HOME

Fusible web, aluminum foil, red
thread, and a safety pin

TECHNIQUES YOU'LL NEED

Fusible Products (pg. 98)
Appliqué (pg. 99)
Painting (pg. 100)

*D*elight a culinary whiz with this
cheery Christmas apron. Gold glitter
paint, red button "berries," and a plaid
bow trim a wreath of fused-on silk holly
leaves for our handy kitchen accessory.

HOLLY WREATH APRON

1. Wash, dry, and press apron.

2. Make appliqués from leaves. Arrange
and fuse leaves to apron.

3. Paint veins on leaves; paint over some
edges of leaves.

4. Sew buttons among leaves for berries.
Tie ribbon into a bow; trim ends. Use safety
pin on wrong side of apron to pin bow to
apron.

"SUGAR & SPICE" SWEATSHIRT

WHAT TO BUY

Ecru sweatshirt
1/4 yd fabric for gingerbread boys
3 approx. 1" x 15" torn fabric
    strips for bows
Red and green embroidery floss

THINGS YOU HAVE AT HOME

Tracing paper, transfer paper, stylus, fusible interfacing, thread to match sweatshirt and buttons, small sharp scissors, embroidery needle, 6 small and 3 large buttons, and a removable fabric marking pen

TECHNIQUES YOU'LL NEED

Patterns (pg. 98)
Cross Stitch (pg. 102)
Embroidery (pg. 103)

Treat a friend to our sweet "sugar and spice" sweatshirt. Reverse appliqués, torn fabric-strip bows, and decorative stitching provide whimsical appeal!

REVERSE APPLIQUÉ SWEATSHIRT

1. Wash, dry, and press shirt and appliqué fabric.

2. Transfer 3 gingerbread boys (pg. 123) to shirt. Use fabric marking pen to write "Sugar And Spice makes Christmas so nice" on shirt.

3. Fuse interfacing to wrong side of brown fabric. Cut three 5" x 7" pieces from fabric. With right side of fabric facing wrong side of sweatshirt, pin 1 fabric piece behind each gingerbread boy shape. Sewing along transferred lines, sew fabric pieces to sweatshirt.

4. Cutting about 1/4" inside sewn lines through sweatshirt only, use scissors to cut away center of each shape. To fringe raw edges, clip sweatshirt close to sewn lines.

(Continued on pg. 83)

79

SILK RIBBON WREATH PINS

WHAT TO BUY

Package of 2 Bucilla® Silk Ribbon
Embroidery Heart Brooch Pins
One 3 yd package each red (49)
and green (19) YLI 7mm silk
ribbon and 1 skein each red
(347) and green (562) DMC
embroidery floss (see Stitch
Guide, pg. 123)
Two 1" long pin backs

THINGS YOU HAVE AT HOME

2 approx. 4" square muslin
scraps, white tissue paper, batting,
lightweight cardboard, felt scraps
for backing, embroidery needle
with large eye, tweezers (if
needed), and glue

TECHNIQUES YOU'LL NEED

Embroidery (pg. 103)
Silk Ribbon Embroidery (pg. 103)

Hand stitched from the heart, these beautiful pins embroidered with silk ribbon will be cherished by those who receive them. The lovely tokens can be easily finished in an evening!

SILK EMBROIDERED PINS

1. (**Note:** Heart brooches are the only items used from kit; set remaining kit components aside for another use.) Lightly draw around 1 heart brooch on 1 muslin scrap. Trace embroidery pattern (pg. 123) onto tissue paper; cut out pattern about 1" outside design. Pin pattern at center of drawn heart on muslin. Referring to Stitch Guide (pg. 123), stitch design over pattern on muslin. Using tweezers if necessary, remove pattern from stitching.

2. Draw around heart brooch on batting, cardboard, and felt. Cut out shapes just inside drawn hearts. Cut out stitched piece about 1/4" outside drawn heart.

3. Center batting heart and cardboard heart on back of stitched piece; fold and glue edges of stitched piece to back, clipping curves as needed. Glue felt heart and pin back to back of stitched piece. Glue heart brooch to front.

CHRISTMAS CUFFS

WHAT TO BUY

3 pair bobby socks with fine
   ribbing (we used white)
Embroidery floss (see color key,
   pg. 83)
1/8 yd 16-mesh waste canvas

THINGS YOU HAVE AT HOME

Masking tape, thread, embroidery
needle, spray bottle filled with
water, and tweezers

TECHNIQUES YOU'LL NEED

Cross Stitch (pg. 102)

Give several friends a toe-tapping Christmas with these cheery cross-stitched socks. The colorful cuff designs are easy to stitch, and they'll surely inspire holiday spirit!

CROSS-STITCHED SOCKS

1. Fold down sock cuff to desired position. Stitching through both layers, baste waste canvas to cuff.

2. Referring to chart and color key (pg. 83), work design over waste canvas, using 2 strands of floss for Cross Stitch and 1 for Backstitch.

3. Remove waste canvas.

COZY HAT & MITTENS
(Continued from pg. 72)

Row 8: Ch 1, turn; sc in first 28 sc, sc in end of first row of last Green stripe and in remaining 10 sc of previous Ecru stripe: 39 sc.

Row 9: Ch 1, turn; sc in same st and in each sc across changing to Green in last sc.

Repeat Rows 2-9 until piece measures 18" from beginning ch, ending by working Row 8. Do **not** finish off.

JOINING
With **right** sides of first and last rows together and working in BLO of sc on last row and free loops of beginning ch at the same time, sl st in first 23 sts; turn Hat right side out; with **wrong** sides of first and last rows together and working BLO of sc on last row and free loops of beginning ch at the same time, sl st in remaining 16 sts; finish off. With Ecru, make a basting seam along top edge of Hat. Pull basting yarn to gather top of Hat; knot basting yarn to secure. Use Green to make a 2½" diameter pom-pom and sew pom-pom to top of Hat.

EDGING
Rnd 1: With **wrong** side facing, join Green with sl st in end of last row, ch 1, sc in end of same row and each row around; join with sl st to beginning sc.

Note: To work **reverse sc**, insert hook in sc to **right** of hook, YO and draw through, under, and to left of loop on hook (2 loops on hook), YO and draw through both loops on hook (**reverse sc is made**).

Rnd 2: Ch 1, working from **left** to **right**, work reverse sc in each sc around; join with sl st to beginning st, finish off. Turn up bottom edge of Hat.

MITTEN (Make 2)
Note: Work in BLO throughout all rows. With Green, ch 81 **loosely**.

Row 1 (Right side): Sc in second ch from hook and in next 9 chs, sl st in next 5 chs, sc in next 23 chs, sl st in next 4 chs, sc in next 23 chs, sl st in next 5 chs, sc in last 10 chs: 80 sts.

Row 2: Ch 1, turn; sc in first 10 sc, sl st in next 5 sl sts, sc in next 23 sc, sl st in next 4 sl sts, sc in next 23 sc, sl st in next 5 sl sts, sc in last 10 sc changing to Ecru in last sc.

Row 3: Ch 1, turn; sc in first 10 sc, sl st in next 5 sl sts, sc in next 23 sc, sl st in next 4 sl sts, sc in next 23 sc, sl st in next 5 sl sts, sc in last 10 sc.

Row 4: Ch 1, turn; sc in first 10 sc, sl st in next 5 sl sts, sc in next 23 sc, sl st in next 4 sl sts, sc in next 23 sc, sl st in next 5 sl sts, sc in last 10 sc changing to Green in last sc.

Row 5: Ch 1, turn; sc in first 10 sc, sl st in next 5 sl sts, sc in next 23 sc, sl st in next 4 sl sts, sc in next 23 sc, sl st in next 5 sl sts, sc in last 10 sc.

Rows 6-12: Repeat Rows 2-5 once, then repeat Rows 2-4 once more.

Row 13: Ch 1, turn; sc in first 10 sc, sl st in next 5 sl sts, sc in next 9 sc, ch 17 **loosely** (thumb), skip next 32 sts, sc in next 9 sc, sl st in next 5 sl sts, sc in last 10 sc: 65 sts.

Row 14: Ch 1, turn; sc in first 10 sc, sl st in next 5 sl sts, sc in next 9 sc, sc in next 7 chs, sl st in next 3 chs, sc in next 7 chs, sc in next 9 sc, sl st in next 5 sl sts, sc in last 10 sc changing to Ecru in last sc.

Row 15: Ch 1, turn; sc in first 10 sc, sl st in next 5 sl sts, sc in next 35 sts, sl st in next 5 sl sts, sc in last 10 sc.

Row 16: Ch 1, turn; sc in first 10 sc, sl st in next 5 sl sts, sc in next 35 sts, sl st in next 5 sl sts, sc in last 10 sc changing to Green in last sc.

Row 17: Ch 1, turn; sc in first 10 sc, sl st in next 5 sl sts, sc in next 35 sts, sl st in next 5 sl sts, sc in last 10 sc; finish off.

With **right** sides together and matching sts, fold mitten in half and whipstitch side and thumb edges together using Green. Turn Mitten right side out.

EDGING
Rnd 1: With **right** side facing, join Green with sl st to end of last row, ch 1, sc in end of same row and each row around; join with sl st to beginning sc.

Note: To work **reverse sc**, insert hook in sc to **right** of hook, YO and draw through, under, and to left of loop on hook (2 loops on hook), YO and draw through both loops on hook (**reverse sc is made**).

Rnd 2: Ch 1, working from **left** to **right**, work reverse sc in each sc around; join with sl st to beginning st, finish off.

TEACHER'S CHRISTMAS VEST
(Continued from pg. 73)

5. Using regular scissors on 1 side and pinking shears on the other, cut ½"w red felt strips to fit along edges of neck, front, and bottom of vest. Overlapping ends, arrange strips on vest and use dots of glue to secure. Use 3 strands of red floss to work Running Stitch along centers of strips. Use 6 strands of red floss to work Running Stitch along edges of armholes.

6. (Note: Refer to Figs. 1 and 2 for Step 6.) For drawstring ties at back of vest, measure about 4" from bottom and about 3½" from each side on inside of vest back and mark with chalk pencil. For slits for each tie, mark 7 approx. ⅝" long lines about 1" apart across back of vest, measuring from each mark toward center. Cut along each mark. Cut two ½" x 17" strips from red felt. Weave 1 strip through slits on 1 side to center. Sew end of strip to vest near slit closest to side of vest. Repeat for remaining side. Pull strips slightly to gather and tie into a bow.

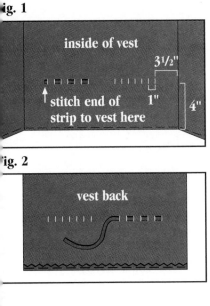

Fig. 1

inside of vest

stitch end of strip to vest here

3½"

1"

4"

Fig. 2

vest back

NIFTY NOEL FOOTWEAR
(Continued from pg. 76)

PAINTED SHOES

1. Use paintbrushes to paint stripes on shoes to create a plaid pattern.

2. For each shoe, cut a small piece of greenery. Tie 6 ribbon lengths together into a bow. Thread 3 bells onto another length of ribbon. Knot center of ribbon length with bells around center of bow and greenery. Move bells to front. Trim ribbon ends. Glue decoration to strap on shoe.

"SUGAR & SPICE" SWEATSHIRT
(Continued from pg. 79)

Trim fabric pieces on wrong side of sweatshirt to about ½" from sewn lines.

5. Use 3 strands of green floss to work Running Stitch over transferred words. Use 3 strands of red floss to work Cross Stitches along neck and cuffs and below each gingerbread man.

6. Sew small buttons to each gingerbread man. Tie fabric strips into bows; trim ends. Sew a large button over each bow to secure bow to sweatshirt.

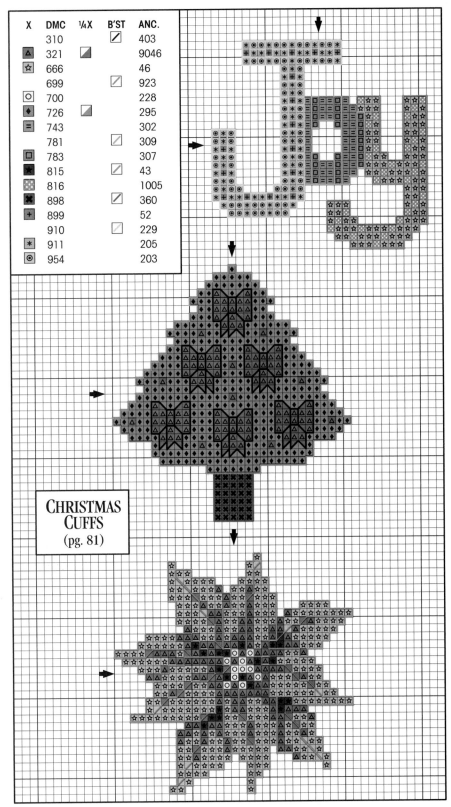

X	DMC	¼X	B'ST	ANC.
	310		◪	403
▲	321	◪		9046
☆	666			46
	699		◪	923
○	700			228
◆	726	◪		295
=	743			302
	781		◪	309
▢	783			307
★	815		◪	43
▨	816			1005
✖	898		◪	360
+	899			52
	910		◪	229
✳	911			205
◉	954			203

CHRISTMAS CUFFS
(pg. 81)

creative
christmas
KITCHEN

*S*pend more time enjoying
the holidays — and less time
worrying about what to give to
friends and neighbors — with
our fabulous collection of fast-
and-fun food gifts. The creative
offerings include savory cheese
balls served on cheery decoupaged
plates, candied spoons in merry
painted mugs, and poinsettia-
embellished gift bags filled with
chewy raisin cookies. You'll even
find crafty presentations for
store-bought treats. Whipping up
affordable Yuletide yummies
and cute containers has
never been easier!

CHEERY CHEESE BALLS

WHAT TO BUY

Decoupaged Plates:
Four 8" dia. clear glass plates
1/3 yd fabric
30" x 25 yd roll clear cellophane
10 yd spool 1/4"w red satin ribbon
4 holly sprigs
Veggie Cheese Balls:
2 packages (8 oz. each) cream
    cheese, softened
16 oz. Cheddar cheese, shredded
1 bunch green onions
1 bunch celery
2 large carrots
Box of butter-flavored crackers
    (16 oz., 4 individual packs)

THINGS YOU HAVE AT HOME

Plates: Foam brush, glue, paper
towels, and pinking shears
Cheese Balls: Garlic powder,
ground red pepper, large bowl,
electric mixer, grater, and
plastic wrap

TECHNIQUES YOU'LL NEED

Multi-Loop Bows (pg. 102)

*D*ecorated with Christmasy fabric, our decoupaged plates and savory Veggie Cheese Balls make wonderful gifts for party hostesses. Once the tasty spread is eaten, the cheery serving dish can be reused year after year.

DECOUPAGED PLATES

1. (**Note:** We recommend lightly hand washing plates after use.) Cut an 11" square from fabric.

2. Use foam brush to apply a thin coat of glue to bottom of plate. Place right side of fabric square on bottom of plate. Working from center outward, use fingertips or foam brush to smooth out wrinkles or bubbles. Use a damp paper towel to remove any excess glue. Allow to dry. Use pinking shears to trim edges of fabric even with edges of plate. Apply 2 coats of glue to bottom of plate to seal, covering edges of fabric.

3. Center plate on a square of cellophane. Place cheese ball on plate. Gather edges of cellophane above cheese ball and knot a length of ribbon around gathers. Form a multi-loop bow from another length of ribbon, knotting ends of ribbon on cellophane around bow center. Tuck holly sprig behind bow.

(Continued on pg. 96)

DELICIOUS ELEGANCE

WHAT TO BUY

Poinsettia Gift Bags:
4 white lunch-size bags
Red poinsettia bush with at least 4
    approx. 5³/4" dia. flowers
Gold acrylic paint
Gold glitter dimensional paint
5 yd spool ¹/2"w gold ribbon
Spicy Raisin Cookies:
Package of spice cake mix
    (18.25 oz.)
Container of frozen non-dairy
    whipped topping (4 oz.), thawed
Package of golden raisins (15 oz.)

THINGS YOU HAVE AT HOME

Gift Bags: Newspaper, small sponge
pieces, paper plates, paper towels,
fusible web, aluminum foil, stapler,
and glue
Cookies: An egg, confectioners
sugar, large bowl, sifter, baking
sheet, wire rack, and 4 resealable
plastic bags

TECHNIQUES YOU'LL NEED

Fusible Products (pg. 98)
Appliqué (pg. 99)
Painting (pg. 100)

Our Spicy Raisin Cookies are packed with fruit and rolled in confectioners sugar before baking, so they're extra sweet and chewy! For an elegant presentation, deliver batches of the delicious treats in our gilded, poinsettia-embellished gift bags.

POINSETTIA GIFT BAGS

1. Sponge paint front of bag with gold acrylic paint.

2. Disassemble poinsettia, keeping top petal section and poinsettia center intact for Step 3. Make appliqué from bottom petal section. Center appliqué on back of flattened bag about ¹/2" from top. Fuse in place. Trim top of bag close to petals.

3. Place plastic bag of cookies in bag and fold top about 4" to front; staple closed at center of appliqué. Glue poinsettia center section over staple. Paint gold glitter dots at center of poinsettia. Punch 1 hole in each side of folded part of bag. Thread a 15" length of ribbon through each hole and tie into a bow at front of bag.

SPICY RAISIN COOKIES

Preheat oven to 350 degrees. In a large bowl, combine cake mix, 1 egg, and whipped topping (dough will be very stiff). Stir in ¹/2 cup raisins. Drop teaspoonfuls of dough into ¹/2 cup sifted confectioners sugar. Shape into 1-inch balls, using sugar to keep dough from sticking to hands. Place balls 2 inches apart on a greased baking sheet. Bake 10 to 12 minutes or until bottoms are lightly browned. Transfer to a wire rack to cool. Store cookies in resealable plastic bags.

Yield: about 5¹/2 dozen cookies

MERRY MUFFIN BASKETS

WHAT TO BUY

Muffin Baskets:
5 small baskets with handles
Ecru felt piece
$1/3$ yd each of 3 red and green
coordinating cotton fabrics
Fruit Spread with Muffins:
Can of whole berry cranberry
sauce (16 oz.)
Jar of orange marmalade (12 oz.)
Jar of pineapple preserves (12 oz.)
Jar of strawberry preserves (12 oz.)
Package of cranberry-orange muffin
mix (18.1 oz.)

THINGS YOU
HAVE AT HOME

Baskets: Glue, fusible web, buttons,
5 rubber bands, and raffia
Fruit Spread with Muffins: An
egg, large saucepan, miniature
muffin pans, wire rack, 5 jars
with lids (we used 3 jars from
ingredients), and 5 resealable
plastic bags

TECHNIQUES
YOU'LL NEED

Fusible Products (pg. 98)
Appliqué (pg. 99)

*Send your favorite college students
back to school with the delectable flavor
of tangy Fruit Spread with Muffins.
Tucked inside quaint gift baskets, the
wholesome offerings will remind them
that there's no place like home!*

MUFFIN BASKETS
1. Tear a fabric strip same width and length
as basket handle; glue to handle. Repeat for
basket rim. Tear a 1" x 18" fabric strip and
tie into a bow around basket handle; trim
ends.

2. Use pattern(s) (pg. 124) to make
appliqué(s). Fuse appliqué(s) to felt. Cut
shape from felt, cutting just outside edges
of appliqué(s). Glue shape to basket.

3. Glue buttons to bow and appliqué.

4. Tear a 6" fabric square to cover lid of jar
of spread. Place square over lid and wrap a
rubber band around fabric and lid to
secure. Tie a length of raffia into a bow
around fabric, covering rubber band.

5. Place jar of spread and bag of muffins in
basket.

(Continued on pg. 96)

SPOON SANTA SACKS

WHAT TO BUY

Spoon Santa Sacks:
6 wooden spoons
White and red acrylic paint
Glossy wood-tone spray
6 brown lunch bags
10 yd spool $7/8$"w ribbon
6 Christmas floral picks
6 jingle bells
Lemon-Date Muffin Mix:
Package of all-purpose baking mix
   (3 lb. 12 oz.)
Lemon extract
2 pkgs (8 oz. each) chopped dates

THINGS YOU
HAVE AT HOME

Sacks: Tracing paper, transfer paper, stylus, paintbrushes, black pen, clear acrylic sealer, buttons, floral wire, wire cutters, and glue
Muffin Mix: Sugar, baking soda, butter, large food processor, and 6 resealable plastic bags

TECHNIQUES
YOU'LL NEED

Patterns (pg. 98)
Painting (pg. 100)
Multi-Loop Bows (pg. 102)

*T*he perfect present for friends who love taking shortcuts in the kitchen, Lemon-Date Muffin Mix bakes up easily for a flavorful treat. Plain paper sacks are topped with adorable painted wooden spoon Santas and multi-loop bows for a whimsical presentation. Don't forget to include the baking instructions!

SPOON SANTA SACKS

1. Transfer pattern (pg. 124) to bowl of spoon.

2. Mix a small amount of red paint with white paint to make light pink. Paint face light pink. Mix a little more red with light pink paint to make pink. Paint cheeks and mouth pink. Paint hat trim, beard, and mustache white. Paint nose red. Paint handle and back of spoon red for hat. Use pen to color eyes and draw outlines and details on Santa. Spray spoon lightly with wood-tone spray, then sealer. Glue button to end of handle for pom-pom.

3. Place bag of muffin mix and baking instructions in bag and fold top about 2½" to front for flap.

4. Cut 2 vertical slits about 1" apart through flap and bag. Thread a 15" length of ribbon through slits with ends at front of flap. Form another ribbon length into a multi-loop bow. Knot ends of ribbon on bag around spoon and bow.

5. Cut stem from pick. Glue bell to pick. Glue pick to bow on bag.

(Continued on pg. 96)

89

MUNCH BAGS

WHAT TO BUY

Plastic Canvas Bags:
1 sheet each white and red
   10-mesh plastic canvas
One 2.5 oz. skein each white and
   green sportweight (3-ply) yarn
Package of green and red tissue
   paper
Caramel Popcorn:
Package of popcorn (16 oz.)
Can of lightly salted peanuts
   (12 oz.)
Container of caramel ice cream
   topping (12 oz.)

THINGS YOU HAVE AT HOME

Bags: Large tapestry needle
Caramel Popcorn: Popcorn
popper, large roasting pan,
aluminum foil, and 2 large
resealable plastic bags

TECHNIQUES YOU'LL NEED

Plastic Canvas Needlepoint
   (pg. 104)

Wintry woodland scenes transform simple plastic canvas totes into festive gift bags. Filled with munchable homemade Caramel Popcorn, the seasonal sacks are super-satisfying gifts for those with a sweet tooth.

PLASTIC CANVAS BAGS

1. Cut the following pieces from plastic canvas: two 51 x 71 threads for front and back, two 28 x 51 threads for sides, and one 28 x 71 threads for bottom.

2. Referring to chart and color key (pg. 125), use Tent Stitch to stitch design at center of front plastic canvas piece.

3. To make holes for handles, cut a small hole in front and back pieces of bag about 5/8" from each top corner (**Fig. 1**).

Fig. 1

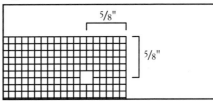

4. Use Overcast Stitch to join front and back to sides; join bottom to front, back, and sides; and stitch around top edges of bag.

5. For handle, cut six 24" yarn lengths. Knot yarn lengths together about 2" from 1 end. Thread remaining yarn ends from right side to wrong side through 1 hole at top of bag front. Braid yarn to desired handle length. Thread ends of yarn from wrong side to right side through remaining hole in bag front. Knot ends at end of braiding and trim even. Repeat for remaining handle on back.

6. Place tissue paper in bag. Place plastic bag of caramel popcorn in bag.

CARAMEL POPCORN

Preheat oven to 250 degrees. Combine 12 cups popped popcorn, peanuts, and caramel topping in a greased large roasting pan. Bake 1 hour, stirring every 15 minutes. Spread on greased aluminum foil to cool. Store in resealable plastic bags

Yield: about 12 cups caramel popcorn

SPICED-UP MUGS

WHAT TO BUY

Painted Mugs:
Plain ceramic mugs
Red, green, brown, and black
DecoArt™ ULTRA GLOSS™
acrylic enamel paint

Cinnamon Candied Spoons:
Package of 1-inch dia. hard
cinnamon candies (7 1/2 oz.)
Bottle of red coarse decorating
sugar (4 oz.)
3 doz. heavy-duty plastic spoons
3" x 4" plastic treat bags

THINGS YOU HAVE AT HOME

Mugs: Tracing paper, transfer
paper, stylus, and paintbrushes

Candied Spoons: Light corn
syrup, baking sheet, waxed paper,
vegetable cooking spray, heavy
small saucepan, and curling
ribbon

TECHNIQUES YOU'LL NEED

Patterns (pg. 98)
Painting (pg. 100)

*A*nyone who enjoys starting the day
with a hot, soothing beverage will
appreciate these cheery gift sets. Plain
mugs are made merry with painted-on
Christmas scenes, and Cinnamon
Candied Spoons are tucked inside for
flavoring coffee or tea.

PAINTED MUGS

1. (**Note:** We recommend hand washing
mugs after use.) Transfer pattern (pg. 124)
to mug.

2. Paint design on mug. Paint handle as
desired. Follow manufacturer's instructions
to cure paint.

3. Place 12 wrapped candied spoons in mug.

CINNAMON CANDIED SPOONS

Line a baking sheet with waxed paper;
spray with cooking spray. Place cinnamon
candies in a heavy-duty resealable plastic
bag; crush with a rolling pin or heavy
object. In a heavy small saucepan, combine
crushed candies and 6 tablespoons light
corn syrup over medium-low heat. Stirring
frequently, heat until candies melt. Remove
from heat (if candies begin to harden,
return to low heat). Place decorating sugar
in a small bowl. Dip spoons into candy
mixture and then into decorating sugar,
pressing sugar into candy. Place spoons on
baking sheet and let candy harden. Place in
treat bags and tie with curling ribbon.

Yield: 3 dozen candied spoons

CHRISTMAS TOFFEE CRUNCH

WHAT TO BUY

Gingerbread Girl Box:
7⅝" dia. papier-mâché box with lid
⅔ yd white rickrack
Two 1"w wooden heart cutouts
⅜ yd ⅞"w red ribbon
¼ yd 1¼"w white pre-gathered
    eyelet trim
Pretzel Crunch:
Package of sliced almonds (2.25 oz.)
Package of flaked coconut (7 oz.)
Package of small pretzels (9 oz.)

THINGS YOU HAVE AT HOME

Box: Glue, red acrylic paint,
paintbrush, fabric scrap for cheeks,
fusible web, 2 small black buttons,
and a black felt-tip pen
Pretzel Crunch: Sugar, butter,
light corn syrup, salt, baking sheet,
jellyroll pan, heavy medium
saucepan, pastry brush, candy
thermometer, and large resealable
plastic bag

TECHNIQUES YOU'LL NEED

Fusible Products (pg. 98)
Appliqué (pg. 99)
Painting (pg. 100)

*O*ur little sweetheart offers a
delicious treat — Pretzel Crunch,
a toffee candy packed with toasted
almonds and coconut! To craft the
gingerbread girl's face, we added a few
simple trims to a papier-mâché box lid.

GINGERBREAD GIRL BOX
1. Glue rickrack along edges on top of
box lid.

2. For cheeks, paint heart cutouts red. Use
circle pattern (pg. 126) to make 2 cheek

appliqués. Fuse circles to lid. Glue 1 heart
to each circle.

3. Glue buttons to lid for eyes.

4. Use pen to draw mouth and stitches
around cheeks.

5. Tie ribbon into a bow; trim ends. Glue
to lid.

6. Press ends of eyelet to wrong side and
glue in place. Glue top edge of eyelet along
side of lid below mouth.

7. Place plastic bag of candy in box.

(Continued on pg. 96)

SWEET CANDY CANS

UNDER $5!

WHAT TO BUY

White, red, and green spray paint
White, red, and tan card stock
    paper
1"w wooden star cutout
Green tissue paper
1 lb. wrapped candies-by-the-
    pound
Wrapped candy sticks

THINGS YOU HAVE AT HOME

3 food cans with labels removed,
white paper, fabric scraps for
appliqués, fusible web, black felt-
tip pen, colored pencils, yellow
acrylic paint, paintbrush, natural
raffia, buttons, and glue

TECHNIQUES YOU'LL NEED

Fusible Products (pg. 98)
Appliqué (pg. 99)

These cute candy caddies are a cinch to craft by spray painting empty soup cans and embellishing them with Christmasy cutouts. To complete the small gifts, purchased candies and colorful tissue paper are tucked inside each can.

CANDY CANS

1. Spray paint can white, red, or green.

2. Use pattern(s) (pg. 126) to make appliqué(s), making angel body appliqué from white paper.

3. Use pen and colored pencils to draw and color face on gingerbread boy appliqué or hair, face, hands, and feet on angel body appliqué.

4. Arrange appliqué(s) on card stock paper and fuse in place.

5. Use pen to draw stitches just outside edges of appliqué(s). Cut shape from paper just outside stitches.

6. Tie several lengths of raffia into a bow and glue to shape. Glue button(s) to shape.

7. For angel, paint star yellow, use pen to draw stitches on star, and glue star to angel.

8. Glue shape to can. Line can with tissue paper and fill with candies.

HEAVENLY COOKIE BAGS

UNDER $5!

WHAT TO BUY

Angel Clips:
6 flat wooden ice cream spoons
3/4 yd 2¹/₂"w gold fringe
Eighteen 4" dia. white paper doilies
6 gold charms
1¹/₃ yds ¹/₄"w gold ribbon
Cookie Wreaths:
Package of 1¹/₂" dia. thin butter
  cookies (12 oz.)
2 tubes (4.25 oz. each) green
  decorating icing and a set of 4
  plastic decorating tips for tubes
Package of small red cinnamon
  candies (9 oz.)
Six 2" x 8¹/₂" cellophane bags

THINGS YOU HAVE AT HOME

Angel Clips: Blue acrylic paint,
paintbrush, 6 spring-type
clothespins, dark pink colored
pencil, black felt-tip pen, and glue

TECHNIQUES YOU'LL NEED

Painting (pg. 100)

*A*dd heavenly charm to gift bags
with our adorable angel clip-ons. The
bags are filled with store-bought butter
cookies that you decorate to look like
little wreaths using piped-on icing and
candy "berries."

ANGEL CLIPS

1. Paint dots for eyes on large end (top)
of spoon. Use pencil to color cheeks and
mouth. Use pen to draw pupils in eyes and
eyelashes.

2. With clip at bottom of spoon, glue
clothespin to back of spoon.

3. Cut a 3" length of fringe. Glue finished
edge of fringe around angel's head. For
bangs, cut a small piece of fringe and glue
to top of head. Trim bangs.

4. For arms and wings, fold 2 doilies in
half. Matching folded edges (tops), stack
doilies together and use a dot of glue at
center to secure.

5. For dress, fold edges of another doily to
wrong side, overlapping edges (**Fig. 1**);
glue to secure. Cut about ¹/₈" from point at
top of dress. Glue top of dress to center top
of arms and wings.

Fig. 1

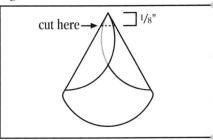

cut here → ☐ ¹/₈"

(Continued on pg. 96)

PLAYFUL PET STOCKINGS

UNDER $5!

WHAT TO BUY

9" x 12" piece of Antique White
   Aida (14 ct) for each stocking
Embroidery floss (see color key,
   pg. 127)
²/₃ yd muslin
Cat and dog treats
Cellophane bag for each stocking

THINGS YOU HAVE AT HOME

Tapestry needle, embroidery hoop
(optional), thread to match Aida
and muslin

TECHNIQUES YOU'LL NEED

Patterns (pg. 98)
Cross Stitch (pg. 102)

Surprise an animal lover (or your own ever-faithful pet) with one of these personalized Christmas stockings. Cross stitched with playful motifs, the small stockings are filled with purchased treats.

PERSONALIZED PET STOCKINGS

1. Referring to chart and color key (pg. 127) and stitching over 2 fabric threads, work design on Aida, using 6 strands of floss for Cross Stitch and 2 for Backstitch and French Knots.

2. Make stocking pattern (pg. 126). Arrange pattern on wrong side of stitched piece and use a pencil to lightly draw around pattern. Cut a 9" x 12" piece of muslin for stocking back. Pin stitched

design (stocking front) and stocking back right sides together. Leaving top edge of stocking open, use a short straight stitch to sew pieces together along drawn lines on stitched piece. Cut out stocking along drawn line at top and about ³/₈" from seamline. Clip seam allowance at curves. Do not turn right side out.

3. For lining, cut two 9" x 12" pieces of muslin. Pin pieces together. Draw around stocking pattern on muslin. Leaving top edge open and leaving an approx. 3" opening along seamline for turning, sew pieces together along drawn lines. Cut out lining along drawn line at top and about ¹/₄" from seamline. Turn right side out and press.

(Continued on pg. 96)

95

CHEERY CHEESE BALLS
(Continued from pg. 86)

VEGGIE CHEESE BALLS

In a large bowl, combine cheeses; beat until smooth. Stir in 1 1/2 cups finely chopped green onions, 1 cup finely chopped celery, 1 cup shredded carrots, 1 1/2 teaspoons garlic powder, and 3/4 teaspoon ground red pepper. Divide mixture into fourths; shape each fourth into a ball. Garnish with sliced green onions. Wrap in plastic wrap and chill 2 hours or until firm. Store in refrigerator. Give with crackers.

Yield: 4 cheese balls, about 1 1/4 cups each

MERRY MUFFIN BASKETS
(Continued from pg. 88)

FRUIT SPREAD WITH MUFFINS

In a large saucepan, combine cranberry sauce, orange marmalade, pineapple preserves, and strawberry preserves. Stirring occasionally, cook over medium heat until heated through. Spoon cranberry mixture into jars. Store in refrigerator.

Preheat oven to 400 degrees. Prepare muffins according to package directions using egg and water. Bake 12 to 15 minutes in greased miniature muffin pans. Transfer to a wire rack to cool. Store muffins in resealable plastic bags.

Yield: about 5 cups spread and 40 mini muffins

SPOON SANTA SACKS
(Continued from pg. 89)

LEMON-DATE MUFFIN MIX

Process 6 cups baking mix, 1 1/2 cups sugar, and 1 1/2 teaspoons baking soda in a large food processor until blended. Add 3/4 cup butter and 1 1/2 teaspoons lemon extract; process until blended. Add 1 package dates and pulse process just until mixed. Divide muffin mix into

3 resealable plastic bags. Repeat with same amount of ingredients. Give with baking instructions.

Yield: 6 bags muffin mix, about 3 cups each

To bake Lemon-Date Muffins: Preheat oven to 400 degrees. Line a muffin pan with paper muffin cups. In a large bowl, combine 1 bag muffin mix, 8 ounces lemon yogurt, and 1 egg; stir until just moistened. Spoon batter into muffin cups, filling each about two-thirds full. Sprinkle 1/4 teaspoon sugar over each muffin. Bake 15 to 17 minutes or until tops are lightly browned. Serve warm or transfer to a wire rack to cool. Store in an airtight container.

Yield: about 1 dozen muffins

CHRISTMAS TOFFEE CRUNCH
(Continued from pg. 92)

PRETZEL CRUNCH

Preheat oven to 350 degrees. Spread almonds and 1/2 cup coconut on an ungreased baking sheet. Stirring every 2 minutes, bake 4 to 6 minutes or until almonds and coconut are lightly browned. Combine almonds, coconut, and 2 cups pretzels in a 10 1/2 x 15 1/2-inch greased jellyroll pan; spread in a single layer. Butter sides of a heavy medium saucepan. Combine 1 cup plus 2 tablespoons sugar, 1/3 cup butter, 2 tablespoons water, 2 teaspoons light corn syrup, and 1/2 teaspoon salt in saucepan. Stirring constantly, cook over medium-low heat until sugar dissolves. Using a pastry brush dipped in hot water, wash down any sugar crystals on sides of pan. Attach a candy thermometer to pan, making sure thermometer does not touch bottom of pan. Increase heat to medium and bring to a boil. Cook, without stirring, until mixture reaches 290 degrees. Test about 1/2 teaspoon mixture in ice water. Mixture will form hard threads in ice water but will soften when removed from the water.

Pour in a thin stream over pretzel mixtur do not stir. Let cool and break into piece Store candy in resealable plastic bag.

Yield: about 1 pound candy

HEAVENLY COOKIE BAGS
(Continued from pg. 94)

6. Fold sides of front folded doily to fron for arms; glue in place. Glue charm between arms. Tie an 8" length of ribbon into a bow and glue to top of dress. Glue back of wings to spoon.

7. Fold top of bag of cookies several tim to front and clip angel to top.

COOKIE WREATHS

Use icing and star decorating tip to pip icing onto cookies to resemble wreaths. Press candies into icing for "berries." Le icing harden. Store cookies in cellophan bags.

Yield: about 5 dozen cookies

PLAYFUL PET STOCKINGS
(Continued from pg. 95)

4. For hanger, cut a 1" x 5 1/2" piece of muslin. Press in half lengthwise and unfold; press long edges to center and refold. Sew along pressed edges. Fold in half to form a loop.

5. Place stocking lining in stocking. Matching ends of hanger to raw edges of stocking, pin hanger close to heel-side seamline between stocking and lining. Matching raw edges and seamlines, pin stocking and lining together. Using a 1/4" seam allowance, sew raw edges together, catching hanger in stitching. Pull lining out of stocking and turn stocking and lining right side out through opening in seamline of lining. Hand sew opening closed and push lining down into stocking. Lightly press stocking.

6. Put bag of treats in stocking.

The Well-stocked

CRAFT ROOM

As clever crafters all know, you can save lots of time and money on a project when you keep a good variety of general supplies on hand. A well-stocked craft room is something that evolves as you collect leftover dabs of paint or scraps of fabric and take advantage of sales. Our editors checked their own workrooms, compared notes, and compiled this handy list of frequently needed items to help you plan your ideal craft room.

Acetate sheets
Buttons
Cardboard: heavy (corrugated), lightweight (poster board), tagboard (manila folders)
Chalk
Cotton string
Craft sticks
Crayons
Crochet hooks
Cutting mat or folded newspaper or cardboard
Embroidery floss
Embroidery hoop
Fabric scraps
Felt scraps
Floral wire: coated, uncoated
Fusible products: paper-backed web and web tape, interfacing
Glue: craft glue, craft glue stick, fabric glue, decoupage glue, hot or low-temperature glue gun, rubber cement, spray adhesive
Hole punch
Ink pad: black
Iron
Ironing board

Jute twine
Knives: craft knife, utility knife
Measuring tools: ruler, yardstick, tape measure
Needles: sewing, embroidery, tapestry (for cross stitch), large tapestry (for plastic canvas needlepoint), yarn (for crochet assembly)
Paint: acrylic paint, dimensional paint, gold paint pen
Paintbrushes: round, flat, liner, fan, foam, stencil
Paper: tracing, white tissue, white typing, stationery, card stock, construction
Pencils: #2 pencil, colored pencils, fabric marking pencil, chalk pencil, grease pencil
Pens: colored felt-tip pens, black permanent felt-tip pens, removable fabric marking pen
Pins: straight pins, safety pins
Polyester batting
Polyester fiberfill
Pressing cloth
Raffia
Ribbon: scraps, curling

Scissors: multi-purpose, serrated-cut craft, fabric shears, pinking shears, small sharp embroidery
Sealer: clear acrylic spray
Sewing machine
Spanish moss
Sponges: compressed craft sponges, small sponge pieces
Stapler
Stylus or ball-point pen that doesn't write
T-shirt form or cardboard covered with waxed paper
Tape: transparent, masking, removable
Tear-away stabilizer (fusible or non-fusible) or medium weight paper
Thread: sewing (to match fabrics), clear nylon
Tools: wire cutters, needle-nose pliers, handsaw, large nail
Transfer paper: graphite transfer paper, dressmakers' tracing paper
Yarn scraps

TECHNIQUES

GLUES

Use the following guidelines to decide which glue or glues to use for your project. Carefully follow manufacturer's instructions when using any kind of glue.

White craft glue: Recommended for paper. Dry flat.

Tacky craft glue: Recommended for paper, fabric, florals, or wood. Dry flat or secure items with clothespins or straight pins until glue is dry.

Craft glue stick: Recommended for paper or for gluing small lightweight items to paper or another surface. Dry flat.

Fabric glue: Recommended for fabric or paper. Dry flat or secure items with clothespins or straight pins until glue is dry.

Decoupage glue: Recommended for decoupaging fabric or paper to a surface such as wood or glass. Use purchased decoupage glue or mix 1 part craft glue with 1 part water.

Hot or low-temperature glue gun: Recommended for florals, paper, fabric, or wood. Hold in place until set. A low-temperature glue gun is safer than a hot glue gun, but the bond made with the glue is not as strong.

Rubber cement: Recommended for paper and cardboard. May discolor photos; may discolor paper with age. Dry flat (dries very quickly).

Spray adhesive: Recommended for paper or fabric. Can be repositionable or permanent. Dry flat.

PATTERNS

Making a pattern from a whole pattern in book: Place tracing paper over pattern and trace; cut out. For a more durable pattern, use a permanent pen to trace pattern onto acetate; cut out.

Making a pattern from a half-pattern in book (shown by dashed line on pattern): Fold tracing paper in half, place fold along dashed line, and trace pattern half; turn folded paper over and draw over traced lines on remaining side. Unfold pattern; cut out. For a more durable pattern, use a permanent pen to trace pattern half onto acetate, then turn acetate over and trace pattern half again, aligning dashed lines to form a whole pattern; cut out.

Making a pattern from a pattern that has 2 or more parts in book (indicated by dotted lines and arrows on pattern parts): Trace 1 part of pattern onto tracing paper. Match dotted line and arrows of traced part with dotted line and arrows of second part in book and trace second part. Repeat until entire pattern is traced; cut out. For a more durable pattern, use a permanent pen to trace pattern parts onto acetate; cut out.

Transferring a pattern to your project: Make a tracing paper pattern. Position the pattern on the project and use removable tape to tape 1 or 2 edges in place. Choose either graphite transfer paper or a dark color of dressmakers' tracing paper for a light project or a light color of dressmakers' tracing paper for a dark project. Place the transfer paper coated side down between the pattern and the project. Use a stylus or a ball-point pen that doesn't write to trace over the lines of the pattern.

Transferring a pattern to a rounded surface: If your project has a rounded surface, clip the edges of the pattern and transfer paper as needed to fit the pattern to the surface.

FUSIBLE PRODUCTS

Protecting your iron and ironing board: When using fusible web, interfacing, or vinyl, use a pressing cloth to protect your iron and a piece of muslin or scrap cotton fabric to protect your ironing board. It may also be helpful to keep iron cleaner handy.

Selecting fabrics: Many fabrics are good for using with fusible products, but light- to medium-weight cottons work best. Be careful when choosing cotton blends — some blends may require a lower temperature for ironing, which may not allow the fusible product to bond.

Testing fusible products: When using a fusible product, follow the manufacturer's instructions carefully to ensure a good bond. Before making the project, test the product you are using on scrap fabric, adjusting conditions as recommended by the manufacturer. If the product you are using does not produce good results with your fabrics or trims, try a different product, fabric, or trim. Some fabrics shrink when pressed at high temperatures, especially when using steam. If this happens when you are testing your fabric sample and a lower temperature is not hot enough to melt the fusible web, choose a different fabric.

sing interfacing under web: When
sing a thin fabric over a dark or print
oric that will show through, fuse
htweight interfacing to wrong side of
in fabric before fusing web to fabric.

orking with layers or heavy fabrics:
longer ironing time may be needed
hen layering fabrics or trims or when
ing heavier fabrics. If using heavier
brics, you may want to use a double
yer of web or web tape. To do this, fuse
eb or web tape to both surfaces, then
se together.

emming a fabric piece: Fuse web tape
ong edge to be hemmed on wrong side
fabric. Press edge to wrong side along
ner edge of web tape.

nfold edge and remove paper backing;
fold edge and fuse in place.

APPLIQUÉ

Making fabric appliqués: Trace
appliqué pattern onto paper side of web.
When making more than 1 appliqué, leave
at least 1" between shapes on web. Cutting
about 1/2" outside drawn shape, cut out
web shape. Fuse to wrong side of fabric.
Cut out shape along drawn lines. Remove
paper backing. If pattern is a half-pattern
or to make a reversed appliqué, make a
tracing paper pattern (turn traced pattern
over for reversed appliqué) and follow
instructions using traced pattern.

Making silk floral appliqués: Remove
petals or leaves for appliqués from stems,
discarding any plastic or metal pieces; use
a warm, dry iron to press flat. Place a
piece of foil shiny side up on ironing
board. Place petals or leaves wrong side
up on foil. Lay a piece of web paper side
up over petals or leaves and fuse in place.
Remove paper backing, reserving backing
to use as a pressing cloth. Cut petals or
leaves from foil. Use backing for pressing
cloth when fusing appliqués to project.

Stitching appliqués in place: Cut a
piece of fusible or nonfusible tear-away
stabilizer or medium-weight paper slightly
larger than design. Fuse or baste stabilizer
to wrong side of background fabric under
appliqué. Use either regular sewing thread
or clear nylon thread for top thread; use
thread to match background fabric in
bobbin. Set sewing machine for a medium
to wide width zigzag stitch. If using clear
nylon thread for appliqué, set machine for
a short stitch length; for appliqué with
regular sewing thread, use a very short
stitch length.

Beginning on a straight edge of appliqué if
possible, position project under presser
foot so that most of stitching will be on
appliqué. Take a stitch in fabric and bring
bobbin thread to top. Hold both threads
toward you and sew over them for several
stitches to secure. Stitch over all exposed
raw edges of appliqué(s) and along detail
lines as indicated in instructions.

When stitching is complete, remove
stabilizer. Clip threads close to stitching.

(Continued on pg. 100)

TECHNIQUES (continued)

PAINTING

Protecting your project from excess paint: When painting on a garment or fabric, place a T-shirt form or cardboard covered with waxed paper beneath the layer you will be painting on to protect the rest of the project.

Transferring a painting pattern to project: If painting a transferred design that has basecoats with details on top, transfer the outlines of the basecoats to project first and paint basecoats, then transfer and paint details.

Mixing paint colors: If you only need a small amount of a certain paint color and you don't want to buy a whole bottle, experiment with mixing basic colors to create the one you need. For instance, you can mix a little red and white together for pink, then add a little yellow to make peach.

Selecting paintbrushes: We have recommended types of brushes to use, but you should use the type that is most comfortable to you to produce the desired results.

Practicing: Practice painting on scrap paper or fabric before painting project.

Basecoats: Use a flat paintbrush or foam brush to paint an entire item or an outlined area on an item with an even coat of paint; 2 or 3 coats may be necessary to completely cover the item or area.

Highlights: Use a liner, small round, or flat paintbrush to paint a lighter area of paint on the basecoat (usually white or off-white), giving the appearance of light.

Liner details: Use either a liner or small round paintbrush or a permanent felt-tip pen to paint or draw details of a transferred pattern or to freehand details.

Dots: Dip the tip of a round paintbrush, the handle end of a paintbrush, or 1 end of a toothpick in paint and touch to project. Dip in paint each time for uniform dots.

Dry brushing: Dip a flat or fan paintbrush in paint, then remove excess by brushing on a paper towel until brush is almost dry. Use brush to apply a very light coat of paint to project.

Spatter painting: Dip the bristle tips of a toothbrush into paint, blot on a paper towel to remove excess, then pull thumb across bristles to spatter paint on project.

Painting with a sponge piece: Pour some paint onto a paper plate. Dip dampened sponge piece into paint and remove excess on a paper towel. Use a light stamping motion to paint item, reapplying paint to sponge as necessary. If desired, repeat with a second coat or other paint colors.

Painting with a sponge shape: Use a permanent pen to draw around pattern on a dry compressed craft sponge; cut out sponge shape. Dampen sponge shape to expand. Pour some paint onto a paper plate. Dip 1 side of sponge shape into paint and remove excess on a paper towel. Lightly press sponge shape on project, then carefully lift. Reapplying paint to sponge shape as necessary, repeat to paint additional shapes on project.

Stenciling: For stencil, cut a piece of acetate at least 2" larger on all sides than pattern. Use a permanent pen to trace pattern onto center of acetate. Place acetate on cutting mat and use craft knife to cut out stencil, making sure edges are smooth.

Pour some paint onto a paper plate. Hold or tape (using removable tape) stencil in place on project. Dip a stencil brush or sponge piece in paint and remove excess on a paper towel. Brush or sponge should be almost dry to produce good results. Beginning at edge of cutout area, apply paint in a stamping motion over stencil. Carefully remove stencil from project. To stencil a design in reverse, clean stencil and turn stencil over.

Sealing: If an item will be handled frequently or used outdoors, we recommend sealing the item with a clear acrylic sealer. Sealers are available in spray or brush-on form in several finishes. Use a non-toxic finish when sealing items which will come in contact with food. Follow manufacturer's instructions to apply sealer.

Painting with dimensional paint: Turn bottle upside down to fill tip before each use. While painting, clean tip often with a paper towel. If tip becomes clogged, insert a straight pin into opening to unclog.

To paint, touch tip to project. Squeezing and moving bottle steadily, apply paint to project, being careful not to flatten paint line. If securing an appliqué, center line of paint over raw edge of appliqué, covering edge. If painting detail lines, center line of paint over transferred line on project or freehand details as desired.

To correct a mistake, use a paring knife to gently scrape excess paint from project before it dries. Carefully remove stain with non-acetone nail polish remover on a cotton swab. A mistake may also be camouflaged by incorporating it into the design.

(Continued on pg. 102)

TECHNIQUES (continued)

MULTI-LOOP BOWS

Making a multi-loop bow: For first streamer, measure desired length of streamer from 1 end of ribbon and twist ribbon between fingers.

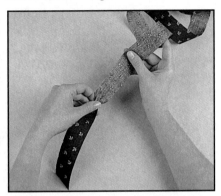

For first loop, keep right side of ribbon facing out and fold ribbon to front to form desired size loop; gather between fingers.

Fold ribbon to back to form another loop; gather between fingers. Continue to form loops, varying size as desired, until bow is desired size.

For remaining streamer, trim ribbon to desired length.

Follow project instructions to secure bow. If project instructions don't indicate a method for securing bow, use the following method: Wrap a length of wire around center of bow with ends at back. Hold wire ends with one hand and twist bow with the other hand to twist and tighten wire. If desired, wrap a short length of ribbon around bow center and glue ends together at back to secure, covering wire. Either use wire ends to secure bow to project or trim ends close to bow and glue bow to project.

Arrange loops and trim ribbon ends as desired.

Making a bow from two or more ribbon lengths: Follow instructions, holding ribbon lengths together.

Preventing fraying ribbon ends: Apply liquid fray preventative to cut edges of light to medium weight ribbon or fabric glue to cut edges of heavy fabric or mesh ribbon to prevent fraying.

CROSS STITCH

Preparing floss: If your project will be laundered, soak floss in a mixture of 1 cup water and 1 tablespoon vinegar for a few minutes and allow to dry before using to prevent colors from bleeding or fading.

Counted Cross Stitch (X): Work 1 Cross Stitch to correspond to each colored square in chart. For horizontal rows, work stitches in 2 journeys.

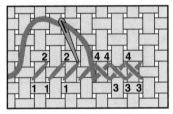

For vertical rows, complete each stitch as shown.

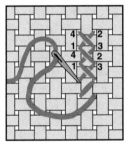

When working over 2 fabric threads, work Cross Stitch as shown.

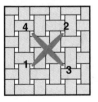

uarter Stitch (¼ X): Quarter Stitches ·e shown by triangular shapes of color in ·art and color key. Come up at 1, then ·lit fabric thread to go down at 2.

·ckstitch (B'ST): For outline detail, ·ackstitch (shown in chart and color key · black or colored straight lines) should ·e worked after all cross stitching has ·en completed.

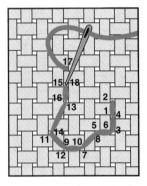

·orking on Waste Canvas: Cut a piece · canvas about 1" larger on all sides than ·nished design size. Cover edges with ·asking tape. Find desired stitching area · fabric and mark center with a pin. ·atch center of canvas to pin. Use blue ·reads in canvas to place canvas straight · fabric; pin canvas to fabric. Basting ·rough both layers, baste along edges of ·anvas, from corner to corner, and from ·de to side. Using a sharp needle, stitch ·esign, stitching from large holes to large ·oles. Remove basting threads and trim ·anvas to about ½" from design. Use ·veezers to pull out canvas threads 1 at a ·me. If necessary, dampen canvas until it ·ecomes limp to make removing threads ·asier.

EMBROIDERY

Preparing floss: If using embroidery floss for a project that will be laundered, soak floss in a mixture of 1 cup water and 1 tablespoon vinegar for a few minutes and allow to dry before using to prevent colors from bleeding or fading.

Straight Stitch: Come up at 1 and go down at 2 as desired.

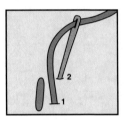

Running Stitch: Make a series of straight stitches with stitch length equal to the space between stitches.

Blanket Stitch: Bring needle up at 1; keeping thread below point of needle, go down at 2 and come up at 3. Continue working as shown.

French Knot: Bring needle up at 1; wrap floss once around needle and insert needle at 2, holding end of floss with non-stitching fingers. Tighten knot, then pull needle through fabric, holding floss until it must be released. For a larger knot, use more strands; wrap only once.

SILK RIBBON EMBROIDERY

To retain the dimensional quality of silk ribbon, be careful not to pull it too tightly or twist it too much when stitching.

Threading needle: Cut an approx. 14" length of ribbon. Thread 1 end of ribbon through eye of needle. Pierce same end of ribbon about ¼" from end with point of needle. Pull on remaining ribbon end, locking ribbon into eye of needle.

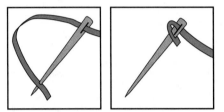

Beginning and ending a length of ribbon: To begin, form a soft knot in ribbon by folding ribbon end about ¼" and piercing needle through both layers. Gently pull ribbon through to form a knot. To end, secure ribbon on wrong side of fabric by tying a knot.

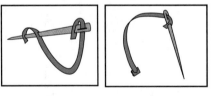

Japanese Ribbon Stitch: Bring needle up at 1 (dot on symbol). Lay ribbon flat on fabric and take needle down at 2, piercing ribbon. Gently pull needle through to back. Ribbon will curl at end of stitch.

(Continued on pg. 104)

TECHNIQUES (continued)

Chain Stitch: Bring needle up at 1; take needle down at 1 again to form a loop and come up at 2, allowing ribbon to twist and keeping ribbon below point of needle. Continue working as shown, securing last loop by taking needle down at 3.

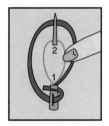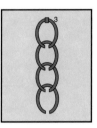

Lazy Daisy Stitch: Bring needle up at 1; take needle down again at 1 to form a loop and bring needle up at 2, allowing ribbon to twist and keeping ribbon below point of needle. Take needle down at 3 to anchor loop.

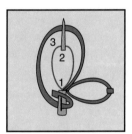

French Knot: Bring needle up at 1; wrap ribbon once around needle and take needle down at 2, holding end of ribbon with non-stitching fingers. Pull needle through fabric, loosely holding end of ribbon until it must be released.

PLASTIC CANVAS NEEDLEPOINT

Tent Stitch: This stitch is worked in vertical or horizontal rows over 1 intersection.

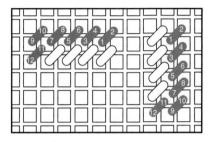

Gobelin Stitch: This stitch is worked over 2 or more threads or intersections. The number of threads or intersections may vary according to the chart.

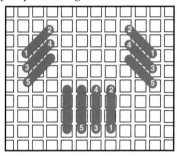

Overcast Stitch: This stitch covers the edge of the plastic canvas and joins pieces of canvas. It may be necessary to go through the same hole more than once to get an even coverage on the edge, especially at the corners.

French Knot: Bring needle up through hole; wrap yarn once around needle and insert needle in same hole, holding end of yarn with non-stitching fingers. Tighten knot, then pull needle through canvas, holding yarn until it must be released.

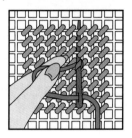

CROCHET

Abbreviations:

BLO	back loop(s) only
ch(s)	chain(s)
dc	double crochet(s)
mm	millimeters
Rnd(s)	Round(s)
sc	single crochet(s)
sl st(s)	slip stitch(es)
sp(s)	space(s)
st(s)	stitch(es)
YO	yarn over

★ — work instructions following ★ as many more times as indicated in addition to the first time.

† to † — work all instructions from first † to second † as many times as specified.

( ) — work enclosed instructions as many times as specified by the number immediately following or work all enclosed instructions in the stitch or space indicated or contains explanatory remarks.

Gauge: Gauge is the number of stitches and rows or rounds per inch and is used to make sure your project will be the right size. The hook size given in the structions is just a guide. The project ould never be made without first aking a sample swatch about 4" square sing the thread or yarn, hook, and stitch ecified. Measure the swatch, counting itches and rows carefully. If your swatch smaller than what is specified in the structions, try again with a larger hook; it's larger, try again with a smaller one. eep trying until you find the size hook at will give you the specified gauge.

ingle crochet (sc): Insert hook in itch or space indicated, YO and pull up loop, YO and draw through both loops n hook.

ouble crochet (dc): YO, insert hook n stitch or space indicated, YO and pull p a loop, YO and draw through 2 loops n hook. YO and draw though remaining loops on hook.

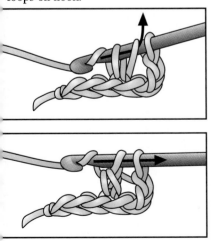

Back loops only (BLO): When instructed to work in back loops only, work in loop indicated by arrow.

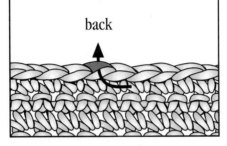

Free loops of a chain: When instructed to work in free loops of a chain, work in loop indicated by arrow.

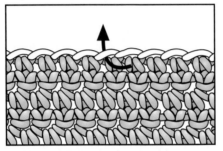

Joining with sc: When instructed to join with sc, begin with a slip knot on hook. Insert hook in specified stitch or space and pull up a loop, YO and draw through both loops on hook.

Changing colors: To change colors, work last sc before color change to last step (2 loops on hook), with new color, YO and pull through; drop old color.

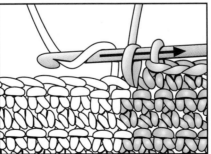

Making a pom-pom: Cut a 3" square of cardboard. Wind yarn around cardboard about 100 times. Carefully slip the yarn off the cardboard and firmly knot an 18" length of yarn around the middle. Leave yarn ends long enough to attach the pom-pom. Cut the loops on both ends and trim the pom-pom into a smooth ball. Fluff pom-pom by rolling between hands. Use yarn ends to attach pom-pom to project.

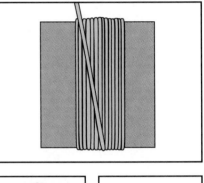

Finishing hints: Good finishing techniques make a big difference in the quality of the finished piece. Make a habit of weaving in loose ends as you work. To keep loose ends from showing, always weave them back through several stitches or work over them. When ends are secure, clip them off close to work.

PATTERNS

PRETTY POINSETTIA COASTERS
(pg. 17)

COLOR KEY
- red
- green
- white
- gold French Knot

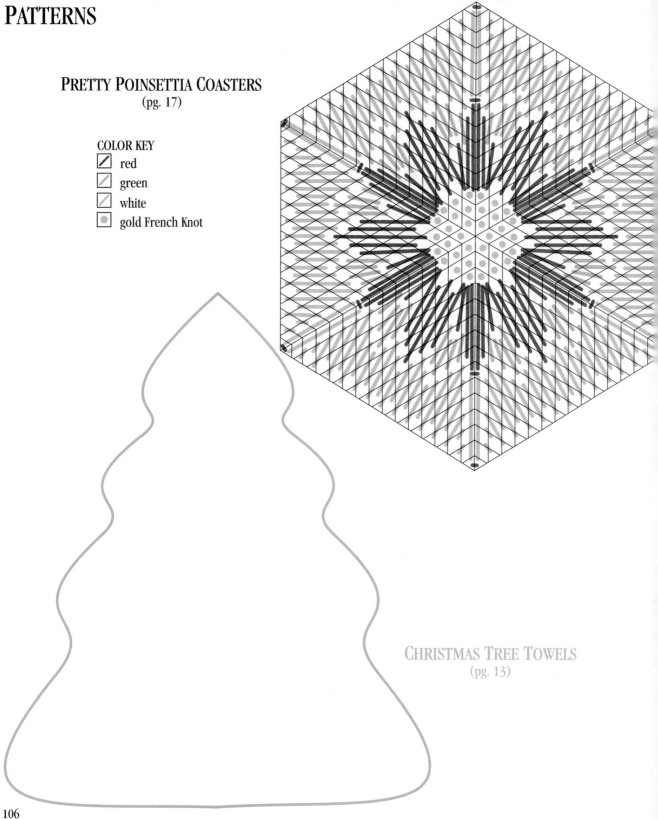

CHRISTMAS TREE TOWELS
(pg. 13)

ANGEL WALL QUILT
(pg. 18)

LEAF
(make 8)

BERRY
(make 12)

LARGE STAR
(make 1)

ANGEL
(make 2 of each
shape, 1 in reverse)

SNOWDRIFT
(make 2)

BORDER STAR
(make 4)

STARRY NIGHT
PILLOWCASE
(pg. 19)

STARS
(make 1 of each)

ANGEL
(make 2 of
each shape)

TREE
(make 4)

PATTERNS (continued)

ANGEL DRESS-UP SET
(pg. 22)

SANTA
COUNTDOWN
(pg. 24)

cut face, hat trim,
pom-pom, mustache,
and beard from
white foam

cut hat, nose, and
coat from red foam

cut mittens
from black foam

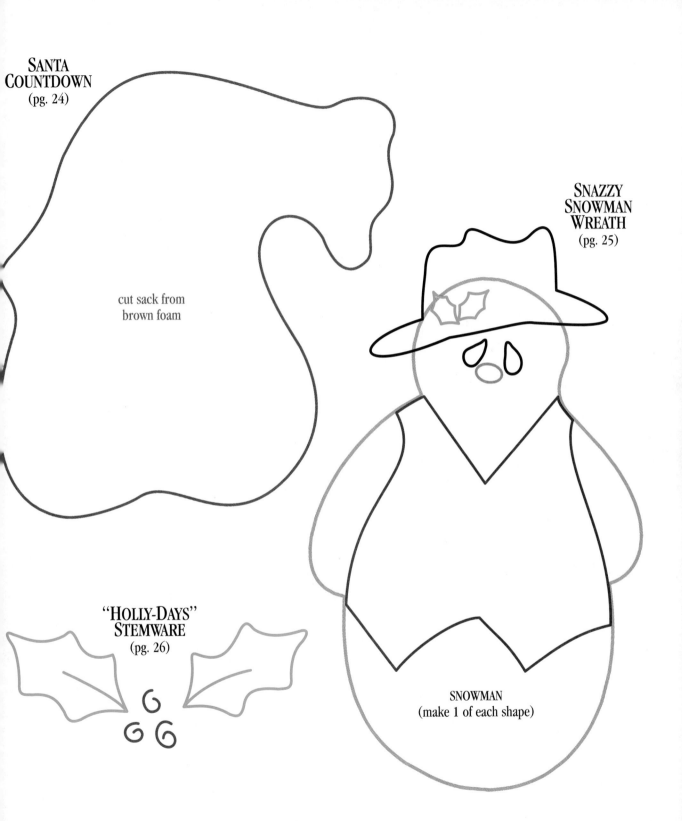

SANTA
COUNTDOWN
(pg. 24)

cut sack from
brown foam

SNAZZY
SNOWMAN
WREATH
(pg. 25)

"HOLLY-DAYS"
STEMWARE
(pg. 26)

SNOWMAN
(make 1 of each shape)

PATTERNS (continued)

CHEERY
TABLE RUNNER
(pg. 27)

make 2 of
each shape
except antlers
and eyes

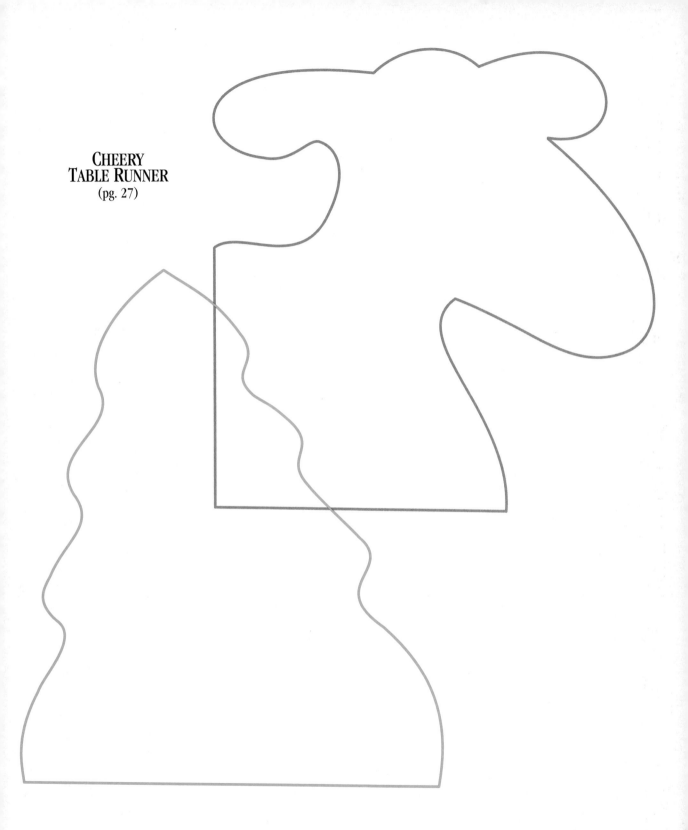

CHEERY
TABLE RUNNER
(pg. 27)

PATTERNS (continued)

SANTA BEAR
(pg. 28)

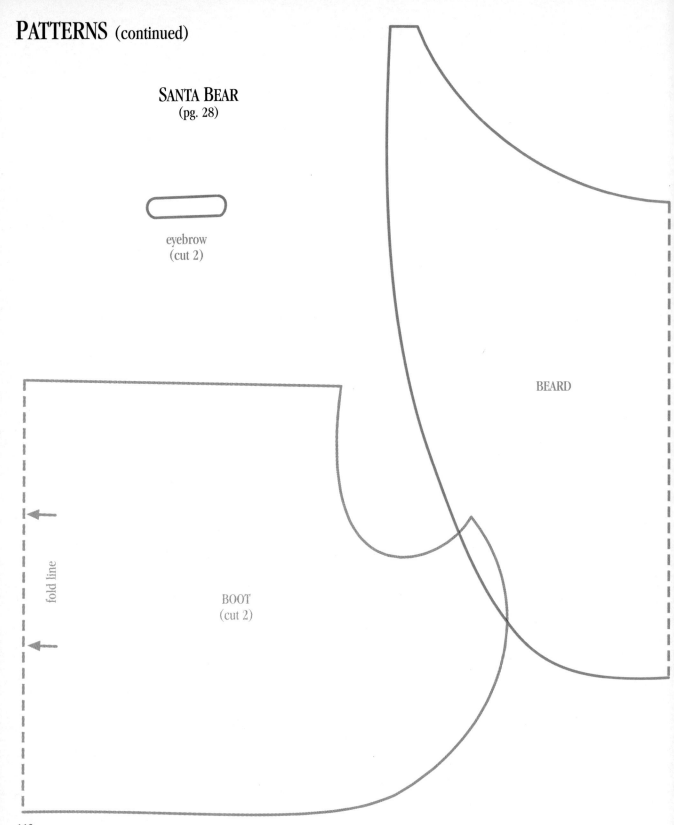

eyebrow
(cut 2)

BEARD

fold line

BOOT
(cut 2)

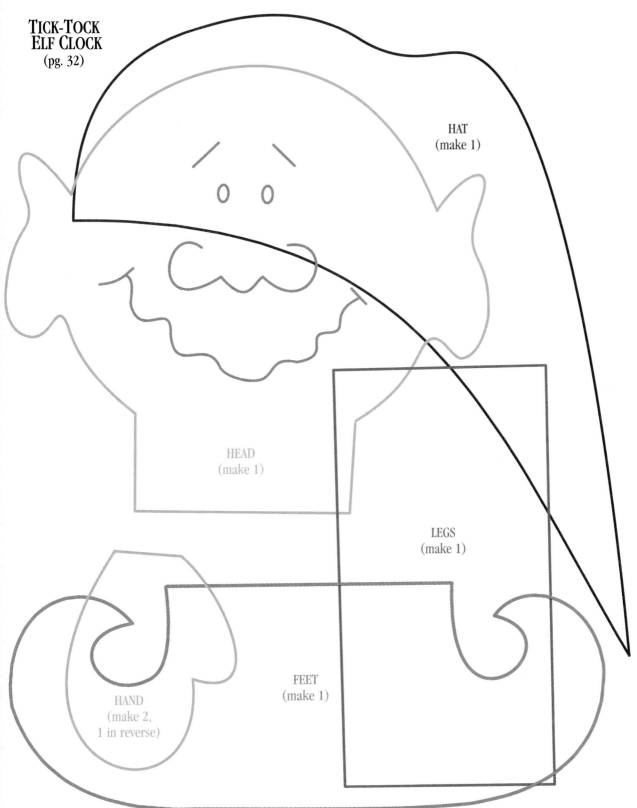

TICK-TOCK
ELF CLOCK
(pg. 32)

HAT
(make 1)

HEAD
(make 1)

LEGS
(make 1)

HAND
(make 2,
1 in reverse)

FEET
(make 1)

PATTERNS (continued)

CHRISTMAS
GROWTH CHART
(pg. 30)

SANTA

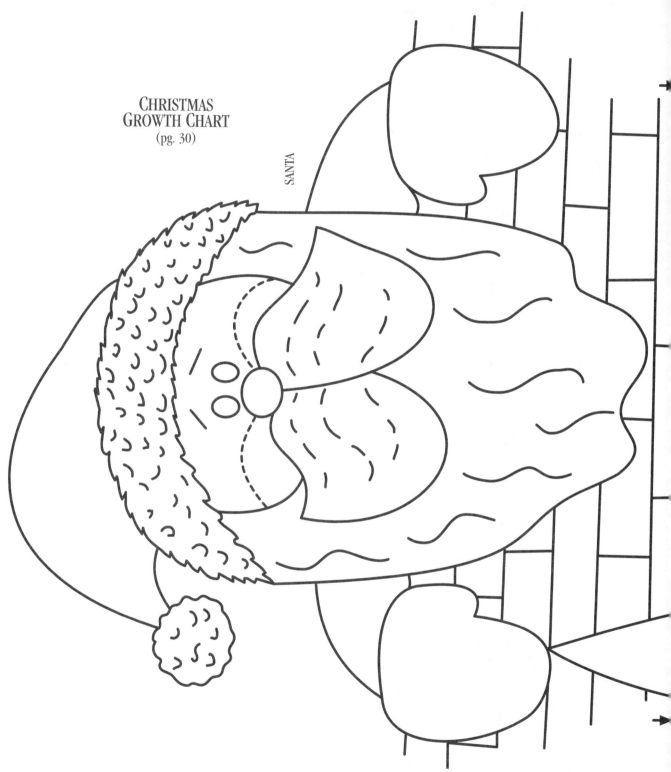

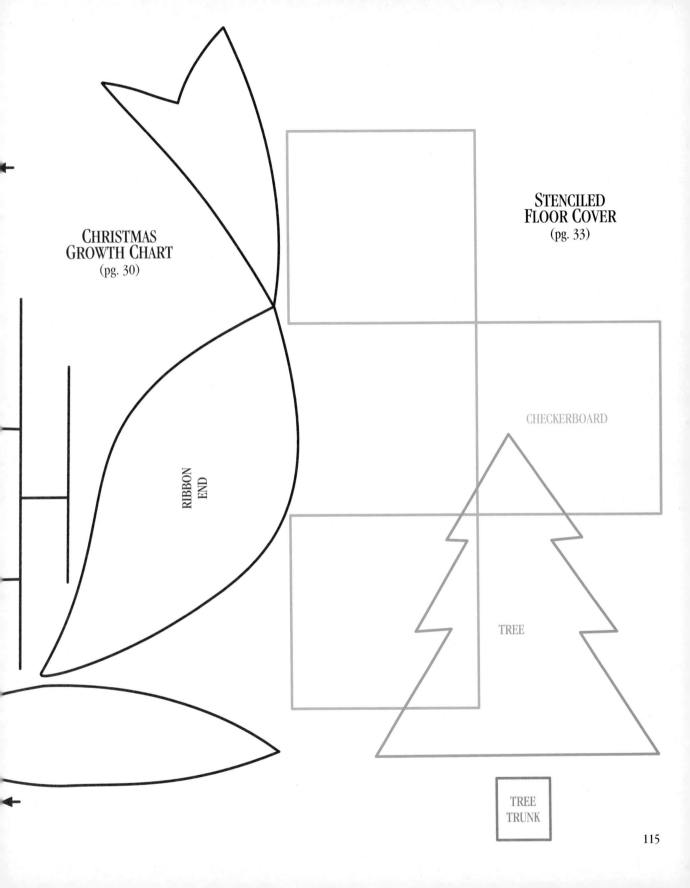

CHRISTMAS
GROWTH CHART
(pg. 30)

RIBBON
END

STENCILED
FLOOR COVER
(pg. 33)

CHECKERBOARD

TREE

TREE
TRUNK

PATTERNS (continued)

FESTIVE
PHOTO MAT
(pg. 35)

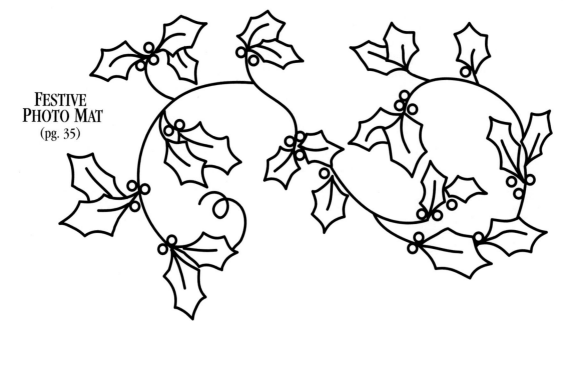

"BABY'S FIRST"
ALBUM
(pg. 37)

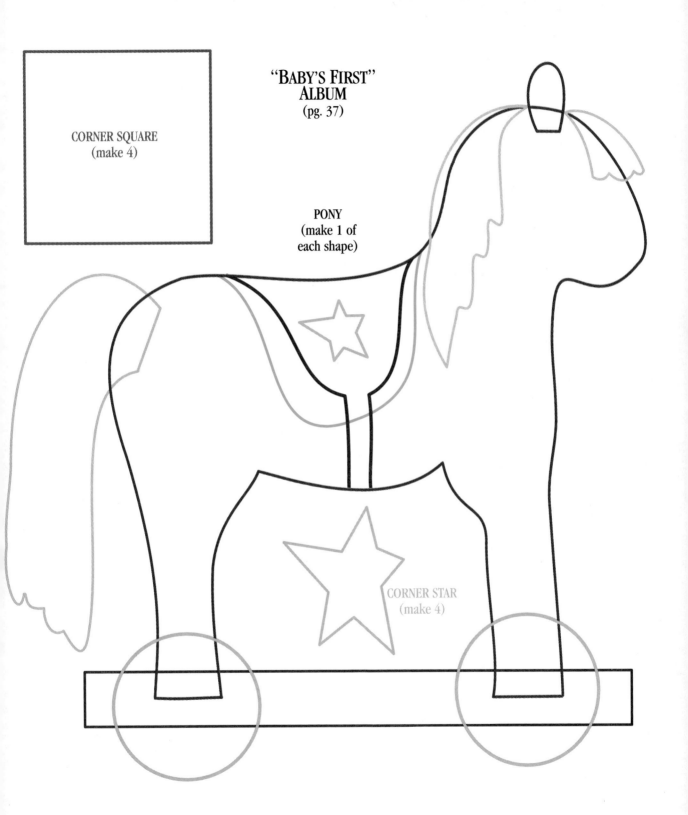

"BABY'S FIRST"
ALBUM
(pg. 37)

CORNER SQUARE
(make 4)

PONY
(make 1 of
each shape)

CORNER STAR
(make 4)

PATTERNS (continued)

BREAD WARMER BASKET
AND CHARMING BIBS
(pgs. 36 and 59)

TREE

MOON

STAR

COUNTRY
STOCKING
(pg. 39)

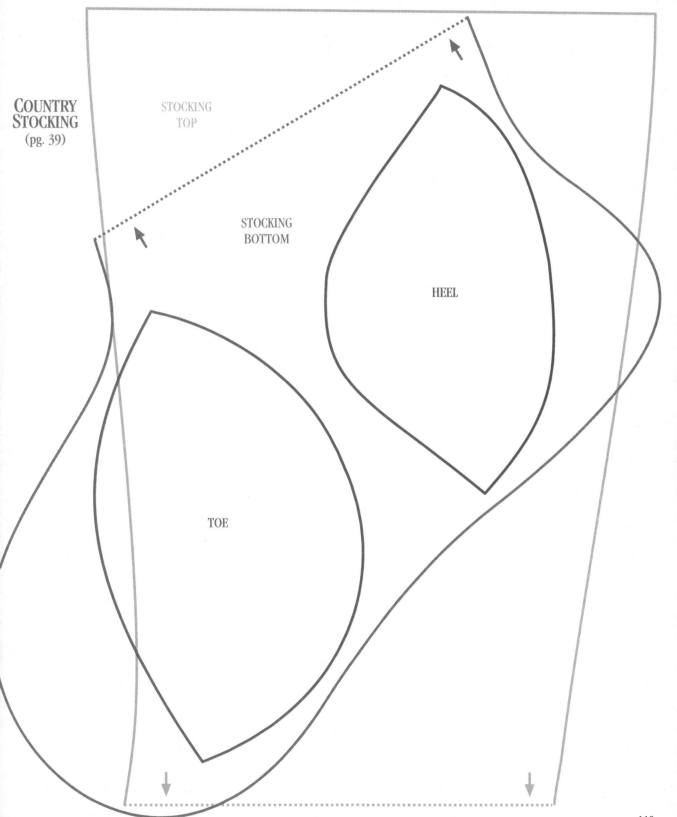

COUNTRY
STOCKING
(pg. 39)

STOCKING
TOP

STOCKING
BOTTOM

HEEL

TOE

PATTERNS (continued)

"NO POUTING ZONE"
SIGNS
(pg. 58)

MERRY MINI
STOCKINGS
(pg. 55)

SNOWMAN

STOCKING
(cut 2 stocking
shapes and 1 of each
remaining shape)

"LET IT SNOW" DOOR
PILLOWS AND EMBELLISHED
PAPER FRAMES
(pgs. 57 and 64)

STAR
(make 4)

POM-POM

SCARF
END

SNOWMAN
FRAME

EMBELLISHED
PAPER FRAMES
(pg. 64)

HOLLY FRAME

120

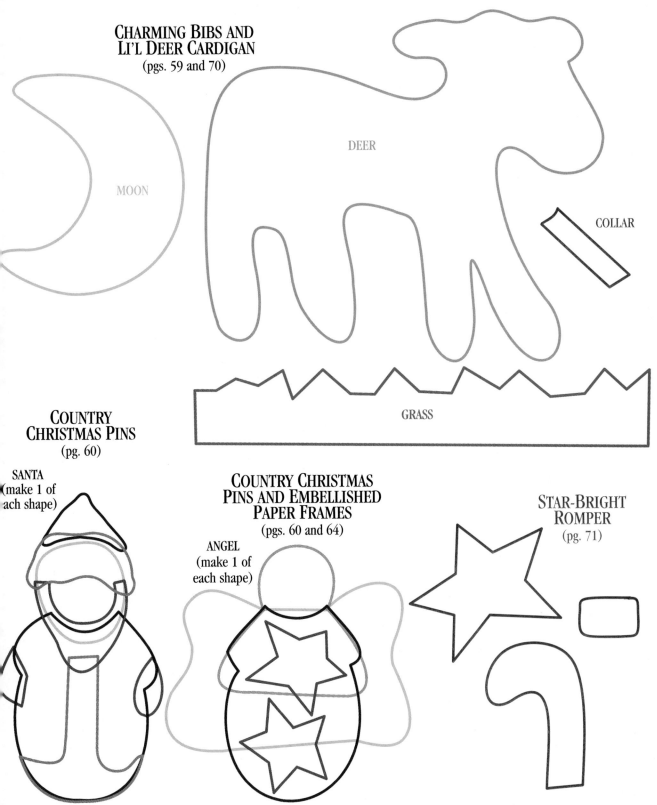

CHARMING BIBS AND
LI'L DEER CARDIGAN
(pgs. 59 and 70)

DEER

MOON

COLLAR

GRASS

COUNTRY
CHRISTMAS PINS
(pg. 60)

SANTA
(make 1 of
each shape)

COUNTRY CHRISTMAS
PINS AND EMBELLISHED
PAPER FRAMES
(pgs. 60 and 64)

ANGEL
(make 1 of
each shape)

STAR-BRIGHT
ROMPER
(pg. 71)

121

PATTERNS (continued)

"COOL"
SNOWMEN VEST
(pg. 74)

SNOWMEN
(cut 1 of each shape)

SILK RIBBON
WREATH PINS
(pg. 80)

CHEEK/COAL
(make 2 for cheeks
and 3 for coal)

STITCH GUIDE			
STITCH NAME	SYMBOL	YLI	DMC
Chain Stitch	◯	19	—
Lazy Daisy Stitch	◯	49	—
Japanese Ribbon Stitch	•—	49	—
Straight Stitch	—	49	—
	—	—	562
French Knot	•	—	347

123

PATTERNS (continued)

MERRY MUFFIN
BASKETS
(pg. 88)

SPOON
SANTA SACKS
(pg. 89)

SPICED-UP MUGS
(pg. 91)

MUNCH BAGS
(pg. 90)

COLOR KEY

⬜ white
⬜ green

PATTERNS (continued)

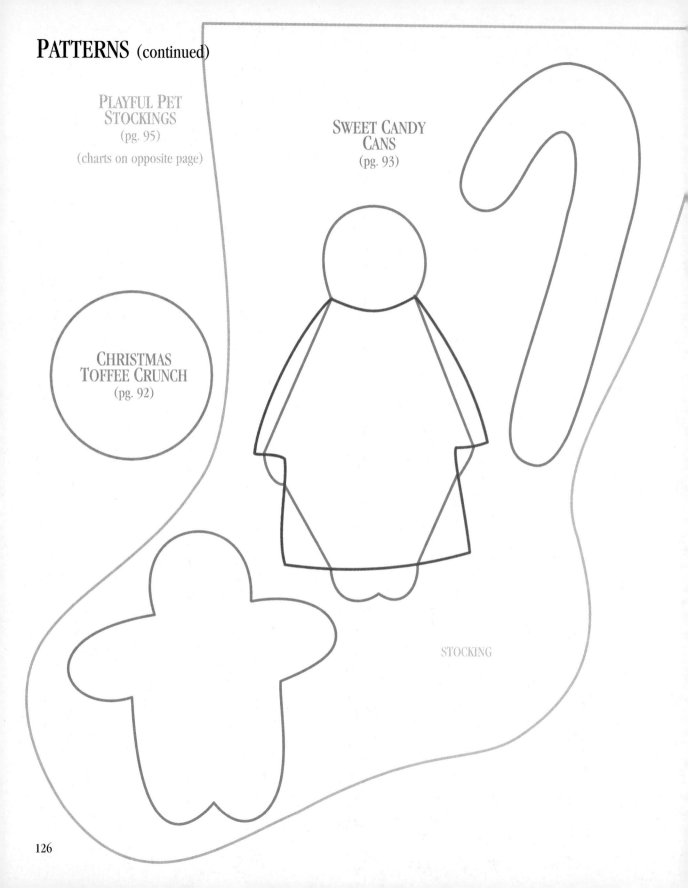

PLAYFUL PET
STOCKINGS
(pg. 95)

(charts on opposite page)

SWEET CANDY
CANS
(pg. 93)

CHRISTMAS
TOFFEE CRUNCH
(pg. 92)

STOCKING

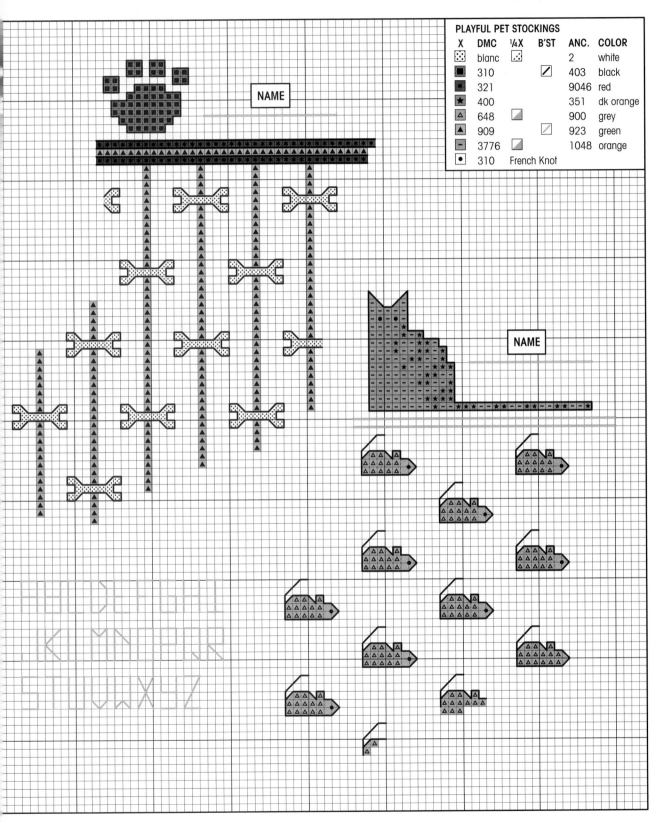

CREDITS

We want to extend a warm *thank you* to the generous people who allowed us to photograph our projects in their homes: James and Joan Adams, Dr. Dan and Sandra Cook, Mike and Jodie Davis, Shirley Held, Charles and Peg Mills, Duncan and Nancy Porter, and Ron and Becky Werle.

To Magna IV Color Imaging of Little Rock, Arkansas, we say thank you for the superb color reproduction and excellent pre-press preparation.

We especially want to recognize photographers Mark Mathews, Larry Pennington, Karen Shirey, and Ken West of Peerless Photography, and Jerry R. Davis of Jerry Davis Photography, all of Little Rock, Arkansas, for their time, patience, and excellent work.

To the talented people who helped in the creation of the following projects in this book, we extend a special word of thanks:

- *Poinsettia Coaster Set,* page 17: Sally Ann Townsend
- *Crocheted Angels,* page 50: Anne Halliday
- *Holiday Faces Ornaments,* page 65: Terrie Lee Steinmeyer
- *Crocheted Hat and Mittens,* page 72: Carol L. Jensen
- *Cross-Stitched Socks,* page 81: Holly DeFount for Kooler Design Studio
- *Plastic Canvas Bags,* page 90: Polly Carbonari
- *Personalized Pet Stockings,* page 95: Jane Chandler

Our sincere appreciation also goes to the people who assisted in making and testing the projects in this book: Lois Allen, Amy Bassett, Michelle E. Goodrich, Kathleen Hardy, and Wanda Hopkins.

Leisure Arts would like to thank Viking Husqvarna Sewing Machine Company of Cleveland, Ohio, for providing the sewing machines used to make some of the projects in this book.